RELIGIOUS
KNIVES

RELIGIOUS KNIVES

Historical and Psychological Dimensions of International Terrorism

JOUNI SUISTOLA, PHD
AND VAMIK D. VOLKAN, MD

PITCHSTONE PUBLISHING
DURHAM, NORTH CAROLINA

Pitchstone Publishing
Durham, North Carolina
www.pitchstonepublishing.com

10 9 8 7 6 5 4 3 2 1

Library of Congress Cataloging-in-Publication Data

Names: Suistola, Jouni, author. | Volkan, Vamik D., 1932- author.
Title: Religious knives : historical and psychological dimensions of
    international terrorism / Jouni Suistola, PhD and Vamik D. Volkan, MD.
Description: Durham, North Carolina : Pitchstone Publishing, [2017] |
    Includes bibliographical references and index.
Identifiers: LCCN 2017024480| ISBN 9781634311304 (pbk. : alk. paper) | ISBN
    9781634311311 (epub) | ISBN 9781634311328 (epdf) | ISBN 9781634311335
    (mobi)
Subjects: LCSH: Terrorism—History. | Islamic fundamentalism—History.
Classification: LCC HV6431 .S8345 2017 | DDC 363.325—dc23
LC record available at https://lccn.loc.gov/2017024480

CONTENTS

For Anja Suistola and Elizabeth Volkan

PREFACE

WE ARE ALL CHILDREN OF WAR

In a *Washington Post* article Lynne Duke (2006) reported that during former US President Bill Clinton's Global Initiative meeting that took place in New York from September 20 to 22, 2006, Archbishop Desmond Tutu made the following statement: "Religion is like a knife. If you use it to slice bread, it is good. If you use it to slice off someone hand, it is bad." At the present time we see people belonging to an extreme jihadist group calling itself the Islamic State of Iraq and al-Sham (ISIS) or Islamic State (IS) actually using knifes to cut off heads. They are not the first group in history to commit such horrific actions. The Zealots, the Assassins and the Thuggee, all ancient terrorist groups, were in essence religious groups— Jewish, Shi'ite and Kali worshippers. All committed brutal murders. According to many estimates, the Thuggee killed hundreds of thousands of people, with at least one suggesting up to two million. There are many other stories in history of killing in the name of religion. When the Crusaders conquered Jerusalem in 1099, they killed about 10,000 Muslims at Temple Mount and a huge number of Jews and Eastern Christians throughout Jerusalem. A Medieval document, *Gesta Francorum*, describes how people "waded in blood up to their ankles" at Temple Mount.

The aim of this book is to increase our understanding of terrorism by looking at it from three combined perspectives: historic, psychoanalytic and systemic. We will look at factors that disturb the well-being of societies, especially factors that cause terrorism. We will question what it is in human nature that allows people, in small or large groups or as lone wolves, to terrorize and kill the Other, including innocent ones. We will examine why the "method" of involvement in war, warlike situations, terrorism and counterterrorism takes different courses during different times in history. We will focus on societal transformations, which affect not only adult populations but also children and youth and future generations (Kaufman, Rizzini, Wilson, and Bush 2002). We will explain the obstacles against peaceful social transformations.

While studying violence we will pay special attention to the role of religion in such events. There are many individuals who, like Desmond Tutu, devote their lives to their Gods and for peace. There are millions and millions of people in every part of the world whose religious beliefs propel them to do good deeds. We wanted to state this simple truth right away to bring to the reader's attention that, by associating religion with unspeakable horrors, we are not minimizing the positive aspects of religion, and we are not questioning individuals' religious beliefs. When humiliating, maiming or killing the Other are carried out in the name of Gods, it is difficult to explore and write about the negative use of religion; it is as if exploring the negative use of religion makes one "anti-religion." Such a label may turn many people away from joining the investigation of how religion "hijacks" humankind's capacity for violence, as explored by forensic psychiatrist J. Anderson Thomson, Jr. (Thomson 2011; Thomson with Aukofer 2011). We believe that such an investigation is absolutely needed in the twenty-first century in which change is taking place at an unprecedented pace and scale.

During the last few decades, *globalization* has become the buzzword in political and academic circles that personifies a wish and an attempt to attain prosperity and well-being of societies by standardizing economic and political elements and by bringing democratic freedom everywhere in the world. Worldwide economic links, incredible advances in communication, and the availability of fast travel are aspects of globalization. In the twenty-first century we are witnessing the ability of the human mind to create incredible technological achievements, while human nature, including its aggressive aspects, remains the same. Even before we began watching in horror the beheadings performed by ISIS and being exposed to frustrating cyber attacks, we began noticing something else: globalization that includes malignant prejudice, racism, degradation of women, child labor, and an indifference to national and cultural differences never brings about the well-being of the affected societies (Çevik 2003; Kinnvall 2004; Liu and Mills 2006; Morton 2005; Ratliff 2004). Extreme Islamist jihadist terrorism, the tragedy of September 11, 2001 and the Western World's—especially the United States'—response to it, wars in Iraq and Afghanistan, altercations and violence in Africa, the Middle East, Pakistan, Ukraine, Europe, United States and elsewhere, have illustrated that globalization, alongside its positive aspects, has induced a metaphorical question in many parts of the world: "Who are we now?" We see the appearance of this metaphorical question after certain significant historical events, such as war, revolution or the loss or rise of charismatic reparative or destructive leaders. What is new in the current era is the globalization of the "Who are we now?" question. Searching for answers to this question has been accompanied by societal fragmentations and violence. On June 23, 2016, for example, the United Kingdom voted, without violence, to leave the European Union. We believe that this unexpected event too is connected with the psychology of "Who are we now?"

As we are writing this book, we are witnessing what is happening in Syria and learning about terrorist attacks in Anbar, Ankara, Baghdad, Bamako, Brussels, Cairo, Dhaka, Diyarbakir, Istanbul, Jalalabad, Kabul, Kandahar, Lahore, Maiduguri, Nice, Orlando, Paris, Peshawar, San Bernardino, Shikarpur, Tel Aviv, Tripoli, and dozens of other places. Since 2014 a vast majority of such attacks have happened in Muslim countries and 60 percent of all attacks have taken place in only five of them (Afghanistan, Iraq, Nigeria, Pakistan and Syria). Out of 35,000 people killed, 80 percent are from these five countries. During the same period since 2014 almost 450,000 people have been murdered worldwide in "normal" criminal cases. In Europe (excluding Russia), between September 2001 and March 2016, jihadist attacks caused the death of two or more people ten times.

In Russia, meanwhile, between 2001 and February 2014, almost 150 terrorist attacks led to the deaths of two or more people, including the Beslan School massacre in 2004, which led to 372 deaths, most of them school children, and the Moscow theater incident in 2002, during which 170 individuals died.

While in this book we will primarily focus on religiously motivated terrorism, we should remember that throughout history and at the present time motivations for all kinds of terrorist attacks vary. The motivation of the Kurdistan Workers' Party (PKK), for example, which has taken responsibility for numerous terrorist attacks throughout Turkey, is political. Such violent events and governments' responses to them, combined with the new refugee crises in Europe, prove the idealized version of globalization an illusion.

It is generally thought that global transformations, positive or negative, take place along four major dimensions: social, economic, political, and cultural. When there are crises in these transformations, most scholars dealing with international affairs and authorities in governments usually look at a number of "hard" or "macro-level" factors to explain them. One of the traditional approaches in the social sciences is to take two events, such as the unemployment rate and the occurrence of terrorism, and then to calculate the correlation between them. If the correlation is high, the unemployment rate is considered to be the reason for the terrorism. In an economic crisis what comes to our minds first are visible factors such as austere budget cuts, high interest rates, and strict monetarist policies. Bolitho, Carr and their colleagues (2003) remind us that there are "soft" or "micro-level" processes hidden behind the hard and macro-level considerations, and they include psychological ones. They state that soft micro-level factors have been increasingly recognized by economists since the days of Adam Smith (1723–1790), and they focus on the importance of communicating human perceptions and motivations, both within and between societal and organizational groups affected by economic crises. They stated that such communications will improve efforts to combat downward spirals into poverty.

In spite of the optimism implied in Bolitho, Carr and their colleagues' paper, too often macro-level factors of a society's problems overshadow the micro-level factors and the latter are overlooked. This happens despite the reality that sometimes micro-level factors must be taken into consideration if there is to be a reversal in conditions within a society. By analogy, this is like a big machine that requires tiny screws to be in their proper places for it to function well, or even function at all (Volkan 2007). We will examine terrorism and the transformation of methods for killing the Other throughout history and their present-day expressions by looking into not only macro factors but also micro factors, especially psychological ones.

The authors of this book come from two different disciplines and different ethnic and cultural backgrounds. The childhoods of both were affected by violent world events. Jouni Suistola was born in Oulu, Finland in 1946. He studied and taught history in Finland. Vamık Volkan was born to Turkish parents in Cyprus in 1932. Six months after graduating from the University of Ankara's School of Medicine in 1956, he went to the United States. There, he became a psychiatrist and also a psychoanalyst. The two authors have come to know each other's cultural, ethnic and religious customs in-depth since they first met in Oulu, Finland in 1983.

Suistola began learning about Turkey and the Turkish realm in 1976 when he visited the country for the first time. When he started to work at Near East University in Nicosia, North Cyprus in 1994 he had the opportunity to learn about the Cypriot Turkish people and their Muslim customs. Between 1998 and 2007 he was the Dean of the Faculty of Economics and Administrative Sciences at Near East University and, from 2001 until his retirement in 2013, served as the university's Vice-President. Besides educating students from North Cyprus, this university attracts students from dozens of countries, especially from the Near East and Africa. Usually Suistola found himself the only Christian in a classroom filled exclusively with Muslim students. Suistola taught a forty-hour graduate-level class on terrorism for numerous semesters. These teaching and learning events were always intense, but discussions were never aggressive or confrontational. After a session, students would often come to Suistola's office to continue discussion. Many of them inevitably decided to write a master's thesis on terrorism. Some had firsthand knowledge of terrorist or militant Islamist organizations.

For example, one of Suistola's Palestinian students proposed writing about Hamas' foreign policy. When Suistola wondered about the possible sources available for such a study, the student's answer was: "No problem. I am a member of Hamas, and I know all the leaders personally." The student left for his field studies, and Suistola did not see or hear from him for a year. When the student returned to North Cyprus he told the story of what had happened to him when he was away. First, he was jailed for three months in Jordan because authorities there suspected him of being a member of Hamas. When he was released from jail and went to the West Bank once more he was imprisoned again, this time in the West Bank, for another three months and for the same reason. Finally, he reached Gaza and was able to conduct the interviews for his thesis. By the time the thesis was ready, four individuals he had interviewed, including the spiritual leader of Hamas, Sheikh Ahmed Yassin, had been killed by Israeli security forces.

Suistola's own childhood experiences were motivating factors for his study of history, especially war history, and, in the later part of his career, terrorism. Suistola was born less than one year after the end of the Second World War and fifteen months after the last German troops were pushed out of Northern Finland. At that time Suistola's father was the officer in charge of the northernmost garrison in Finland. The war was over, but the destructive traces of the war continued to exist. In February 1944 the Soviet strategic bombers had hit Suistola's hometown Oulu twice. They used incendiary bombs that caused terrible destruction in the city, where the majority of the buildings were wooden. As a result, Suistola's childhood home shared a street with the remains of dozens of houses that had been burned to the ground and had two makeshift bomb shelters in the basement.

Suistola's father began his military career as a sergeant in November 1939 in the Winter War against the Soviet Union that lasted from November 1939 to March 1940. He took part in two of its most famous battles (Suomussalmi and Kuhmo), and during the Continuation War (June 1941–September 1944) he served as an officer.

In the summer of 1941 Suistola's father was a platoon commander in the Finnish IV Army Corps, which had the task of retaking the Karelian Isthmus and land north of the city of Viipuri. In the Army Corps he was serving in a special rapid task force, Light Brigade Tiiainen. On the evening of August 22 his Brigade was only ten kilometers to the east of Viipuri. The Army Corps ordered the Brigade to proceed fifty kilometers to the southeast and prevent the escape of the Soviet troops from the closing encirclement. The commander of the Brigade, Colonel Matti Tiiainen, was from Viipuri, the place where Suistola's father had completed his military service in 1936–1938. Colonel Tiiainen decided to take Viipuri. At that time Suistola's father was the commander of his lead platoon. They did not have time for reconnaissance when they launched the attack the next morning, and they were not aware that at the same time a Soviet Division had launched a counterattack. Eight hours later the Brigade was back where it had started, and four hundred of its soldiers were dead. Colonel Tiiainen died of his wounds three days later. The military career of Suistola's father in the Continuation War finally ended in July 1944 when he was badly wounded. He returned home from the war in one piece, but the signs of the war were deep in his soul. In repeating nightmares he continued to fight the war until his death in 1962.

Suistola's father never spoke a word to his son about his experiences and told his mother only a few things. Suistola knew that his mother kept his parents' wartime correspondence of hundreds of letters in a cabinet, but when his mother died, the letters could not be found. The only thing left was a wartime photo album with a picture taken in the early morning of August 23, 1941. In that picture Suistola's father is standing in front of his platoon as the top man of the Army Corps just minutes before the attack. For Suistola, it has always been impossible to look at the picture without crying, although he did not know the story behind the picture.

Suistola felt that he would not know his father at all without learning more about the older man's military career, and the search for information became a dominate internal force in his life. During the summers of 2010–2012 Suistola travelled extensively in the battlefields where his father had fought. He collected soil from the spots where the 1941 attack was launched and where his father was wounded in 1944. He brought the soil to his father's grave. For Suistola this provided great closure. He began to feel that his father now rests in peace.

Vamık Volkan visited Finland for the first time in 1981 and over the next eighteen years he returned there once and sometimes twice a year. He lectured at universities in Oulu, Kuopio, Helsinki and Turku and also was involved with the Finnish Psychoanalytic Society and psychotherapeutic organizations. He still visits Finland, but since the early 2000s, not every year. Volkan's marriage to a Finnish-American who still has relatives in Finland has played a significant role in his decades-long association with the country and his interest in Finnish culture and customs.

He also connects his study of world affairs, including terrorism, from a psychoanalytic angle to events in his childhood. To illustrate this we will tell the story of his invitation in 2014 to attend a joint meeting in Paris between the American College of Psychoanalysts and a number of French psychoanalysts and to deliver a paper on the children of war with whom he had worked. As a psychoanalyst, Volkan has been actively involved in international relations since 1979 and has visited many areas where wars and warlike situations existed just prior to, or even during, his visits (Volkan 1988, 1997, 2004, 2013, 2014c). He observed children of war with or without parents in places like North Cyprus, Tunisia, South Ossetia and Kuwait and participated in projects designed to help children traumatized by wars or warlike conditions. While preparing his presentation he had a dream in which he returned to his childhood in Nicosia, Cyprus. World War II had begun when he was seven years old. Cyprus was a British colony in those days, and thousands of Cypriot Greeks and Cypriot Turks had joined the British military. Periodically German or Italian war planes would fly over Cyprus and bomb the island's British bases. This understandably caused great anxiety for Cypriots, especially after the Nazi occupation of Crete in May 1941, which gave rise to fears that the Nazis would set their sights on Cyprus next. He remembers that Cypriots were taught how to don gas masks, and they ate tasteless black bread. He had been impressed by the Indian Sikhs who had joined the British military forces and roamed the streets wearing their turbans. Volkan's family dug a bomb shelter in their garden, where his parents, sisters and he often took refuge when alarms sounded night or day, only emerging when the all-clear told them that the danger was past.

As tension mounted over a possible Nazi invasion, Volkan's father purchased a German-Turkish dictionary with the idea that if Nazis came he would try to talk to them and ask them not to hurt his family. As Volkan recalls, his father kept it locked in a large wooden chest. In his child's mind, his father had done something forbidden. This "secret" also convinced him that the Nazis would definitely invade Cyprus and do terrible things to the family. He lived with chronic anxiety. One vivid memory of this time was witnessing an Italian war plane burst into flames above his elementary school in Nicosia after being attacked by a British Spitfire, and then watching the Italian pilot parachuting to the ground.

His parents decided that his mother should take him and his two older sisters to his mother's village (Kambilli, now called Hısarköy) about twenty miles from Nicosia, where they would be safer, as Nazis were unlikely to bomb such a small place. He recalls staying in this village about seven to eight months while his father, a teacher, continued working in Nicosia. Sure enough, small Nazi planes would fly very low over the village where Volkan, his mother and sisters were staying to bomb places near Nicosia. To this day he vividly recalls standing on a hill near the village watching the Nazi pilots in their planes. Sometimes they waved down at him as they flew overhead. After each bombing he would imagine that his father was hurt or dead, and because there were no telephones in the village, he had to wait until the weekends to see whether his father would get off the old bus that brought him to visit the family. Each week Volkan experienced the anxiety of imagining his father's death, and every weekend his father would come back to "life."

The impact of war on Volkan's childhood probably would have been tamed after he started his new life in the United States in 1957 if ethnic problems between Cypriot Greeks and Cypriot Turks had not become critical. Several months after he arrived in the United States, he learned that his roommate during his last two years as a medical student in Turkey, Erol Mulla, who had been like a younger brother to him, had been gunned down. He had gone to Cyprus to visit his ailing mother and when he went to a pharmacy to purchase medicine for her, a Cypriot Greek EOKA terrorist shot him seven times. EOKA was the acronym of the nationalist terrorist organization, the National Organisation of Cypriot Fighters. Their aim was to bring the British rule of Cyprus to an end and establish the island's union with Greece. Established in 1955, their main armed aggression was directed toward the British people and installations. In 1957 TMT, the

Turkish Resistance Organization, came into existence, and EOKA and TMT began targeting Turkish and Greek Cypriots, respectively. The EOKA terrorist, who was never identified, targeted Erol for the sole purpose of terrorizing the ethnic group to which Erol belonged. Volkan was in a new country with no one in his environment to whom he could express his grief and mourning. Thus, looking back, he realizes that he denied his emotional state and his "survival guilt" (Niederland 1968). It was years later that Volkan would fully realize how losing Erol gave him the impetus to study trauma at the hand of the Other and grief and mourning in individuals and societies (Volkan 1981; Volkan and Zintl 1993). Also significant in his life is his marriage to an American whose father was killed fighting the Nazis when she was only six months old. She is an active member of AWON (the American World War II Orphans Network), through which Volkan knows hundreds of individuals who, because of the war, were raised without their fathers (Volkan 2014b).

In his dream, the night before his 2014 presentation in Paris, Volkan was in the hand-dug bomb shelter in the garden of his childhood house. In the beginning of this dream, he was alone and frightened, and then more and more children entered the bomb shelter, which became bigger and bigger, like an unending muddy hallway. He was lost behind them. He noticed that the children spoke different languages and belonged to different races, but they all looked horrified. Reading Jouni Suistola's childhood history above, the reader can easily picture Suistola also in a hand-dug bomb shelter like the one in the dream. Volkan woke up perspiring, a very unusual experience for him since he could not recall the last time he woke up from a dream in such a state.

The morning after visiting his childhood bomb shelter in his sleep, Volkan found himself visualizing and thinking about the children of this dream from different countries and races. Wars or warlike situations have existed from the beginning of human history. Even persons who have no actual war experiences are influenced to one degree or another by mental images of such conditions, due to identifications, transgenerational transmissions and psychological links to their parents' or ancestors' history. He did not need to go far away to places like Kuwait, Tunisia or South Ossetia to find children of war; they are everywhere. He rewrote his paper for the Paris meeting and changed its title from "Children of War" to "We Are All Children of War."

A friend of Volkan's, a well-known Jewish-American psychoanalyst, Henri Parens, was also presenting a paper during the Paris meeting. As a child Henri had escaped from a concentration camp where his parents and most of his relatives perished (Parens 2004). When the time came to make his presentation at the meeting, Volkan felt embarrassed since it seemed that in comparison to his good friend's moving recollections, his war experiences seemed unimportant. This event made Volkan fully aware of why, while we often read literature about the psychological responses of victims and their offspring to the life-long repercussions of war, seldom do we hear detailed accounts of the psychological impact on perpetrators' children and their offspring. Embarrassment, as well as guilt and shame, most likely account for this. On the other hand, Henri Parens was not able to talk about his tragic story publicly until 1999, at the age of seventy. As Peter Loewenberg (1991) and Leo Rangell (2003) remind us, some aspects of a large-group history inevitably induce anxiety. Rafael Moses and Yechezhel Cohen (1993) state that "the wish not to have terrible events be true, not to have them touch us, not to be too closely aware of what took place" (p. 130) is the primary reason we deny or avoid dwelling on the impact of tragic historical events in our lives.

We present our stories from our childhoods here to illustrate that people can give sublimated and even creative responses to troublesome childhood events, often without being aware of what has motivated them. Such studies are necessary to understand better our present world, which is now so contaminated with terror. Henri Parens became an internationally recognized child psychoanalyst. He immersed himself in years of studying infants' aggressive behaviors, found ways to optimize childrearing by means of "formal" parenting education, revised the psychoanalytic theory of aggression, and attempted to find a more factual and verifiable explanation as to why we have wars (Parens 1979, 2011, 2014). Other psychoanalysts—Anna Ornstein (Ornstein and Goldman 2004), Vera Muller-Paisner (2005), Charlotte Kahn (2008) and Paul Ornstein (Ornstein and Epstein 2015)—have similar stories. The authors' sublimated responses have motivated them to study the role of "bad things" in influencing the human mind and activities.

Jouni Suistola became a historian. He wanted to study the history of every stone, so to speak, on the present Finnish–Russian border where his father had fought. Vamık Volkan "moved off the couch" (Lemma and Patrick 2010) and worked for a peaceful world in an attempt to "save" his roommate: If there would be peace between Cypriot Greeks and Cypriot Turks and no terrorism, Erol would come back to "life"!

Egyptian president Anwar el-Sadat's remarkable visit to Israel in 1977 crystallized Volkan's efforts to understand the psychology of international relations. When Sadat addressed the Israeli Knesset he spoke about a psychological wall between Arabs and Israelis and stated that psychological barriers constituted 70 percent of all problems existing between the two sides. With the blessings of the Egyptian, Israeli and American governments, the American Psychiatric Association's Committee on Psychiatry and Foreign Affairs followed up on Sadat's statements by bringing together influential Israelis, Egyptians and later Palestinians for a series of unofficial negotiations that took place between 1979 and 1986. Volkan's membership in this committee and his chairing it three years after becoming a member, initiated his study of enemy relationships, interactions between political leaders and their followers, and large-group identity. Two former U.S. diplomats, Harold Saunders and Joseph Montville, also became members of this committee. This helped Volkan to find useful channels of communication between psychoanalysis and diplomacy. Volkan also interviewed traumatized people in various camps for refugees or internally displaced persons (Volkan 2017) and learned about not only the consequences of war or terrorism, but also what psychological factors may lead to the appearance of wars, warlike conditions and terrorist activities (Volkan 2013). Since 2008, Lord John Alderdice from the United Kingdom, Roberto Friedman from Israel, Gerard Fromm from the United States, and Volkan have chaired a series of meetings involving individuals representing Germany, Israel, Iran, Turkey, Russia, United States, United Kingdom and the West Bank. These meetings, which compose the International Dialogue Initiative (IDI), have been very helpful in examining how people belonging to different large groups perceive political, societal, legal, military and terroristic movements worldwide.

A joint warning by Edward Shapiro and A. Wesley Carr (2006), a psychoanalyst and Anglican priest respectively, tells us that attempts to understand international societal processes may be "a defense against the experience of despair about the world, a grandiose effort to manage the unmanageable" (p. 256). However, we wish to remember a statement by Sigmund Freud (1927): "We may insist as much as we like that the human intellect is weak in comparison with human instincts, and be right in doing so. But nevertheless there is something peculiar about this weakness. The voice of the intellect is a soft one, but it does not rest until it has gained a hearing. Ultimately, after endlessly repeated rebuffs, it succeeds. This is one of the few points in which one may be optimistic about the future of mankind" (p. 53). With this optimism in mind, we hope that the historical and psychological insights offered in this book will prove to be of value in helping to tame massive violent events.

1

MILITARY HISTORY AND TERRORISM

From Conventional to Nonconventional Warfare

In February 2009 President Barack Obama decided to increase the number of U.S. troops in Afghanistan with the idea of defeating the enemy quickly and then withdrawing U.S. forces. During this "surge," between 2009 and 2012, Jouni Suistola had an opportunity to discuss the situation in Afghanistan with an American diplomat who had served there for years. One of Suistola's questions to him was: "How many boots on the ground would be needed to defeat the Taliban?" The diplomat answered this question by stating that "there is no such number." The diplomat's response illustrated the extreme difficulty or even impossibility that a strong conventional military force could defeat a militia organization that utilizes nonconventional tactics. Years earlier the United States faced a similar problem in Vietnam where the enemy consisted of guerrillas, people involved in irregular mini-wars.

The term guerrilla comes from Spanish and means little war. Instead of being involved in major battles the guerrillas split the war into many simultaneous or successive mini-wars. In conventional warfare, choosing the time and place for a battle usually belongs to the stronger party, sometimes even by "agreement" between the warring parties. Waging many mini-wars allows guerrillas to define the time and place of the battles and offers the weaker party an opportunity to hit its enemy's most vulnerable targets and to do so by surprise. They force the stronger party to expand the defense lines to faraway places, even to another continent. During the Vietnam War the guerrillas' fighting lines were extended to Southeast Asia. These factors explain why guerrillas can win a war against a stronger party.

The word "terrorism" comes from a Latin term that means "to frighten" and in everyday language, it refers to using violence against innocent civilians with an aim to reach political, religious or ideological change. It, like guerrilla warfare, illustrates a significant imbalance in terms of opposing parties' power. There is no clear-cut and universally accepted definition of terrorism. Here we will start with an "operational" definition by referring to it as a strategy. Strategy is a general concept that refers to what a party is trying to do and what tactics are needed to reach a goal. The overall aim of terrorism is to achieve a political, ideological, or religious goal through violence and intimidation. The internationalization of terrorism in modern times began around 1970 with Palestinian terrorist organizations, but the September 11, 2001 attacks made fighting against terrorism global. In this chapter we will examine conventional and nonconventional warfare from a historical perspective in order to illustrate how guerrilla warfare and terrorism in modern times have become elements of human affairs.

During prehistoric tribal warfare and during warfare prior to the establishment of organized communities—first states such Sumer in southern Mesopotamia or Egypt in North Africa—opposing groups always used nonconventional or guerrilla tactics (Boot 2013). Irregular armed groups engaged in mini-wars without front lines. The history of insurgent and terrorist groups also goes back to ancient times. In the first century, for example, Jews revolted against the Roman Empire. At the core of the revolt were Zealots, who staged violent attacks against Romans and Greeks. So-called Sicarii (violent or dagger men), a Zealot splinter group, even targeted Jews whom they regarded as "collaborators" with Romans. Perhaps the most notable historical violent figures were medieval Nizari Ismailis known as the Assassins. Their organization, a Shia Islamic sect, was established around 1080 in Persia and fought Sunni Seljuks for power as well as invading Christian Crusaders. The term "Assassins" refers to hashish and carries the implication that the attackers were under the influence of drugs when launching their attacks. Most probably this term came from enemy propaganda. Over the course of 300 years the Assassins murdered caliphs, viziers and also crusaders. Their title gave birth to the modern term "assassination." The Thuggee in India, meanwhile, who operated from the thirteenth to the nineteenth centuries, are perceived as the world's first mafia. They were brigands who worshipped the Hindu Goddess Kali who, among other things, was the goddess of destruction. The word "thug" comes from the name of this group.

Modern conventional warfare emerged in the sixteenth century and was based on two factors: the birth of the modern centralized state and the so-called gunpowder revolution. The gunpowder revolution introduced two major technological innovations to the battlefield, namely a personal weapon called an *arquebus* and a new type of cannon that could be taken into the battlefield. The core of the modern state was mainly based on a deal between the merchant class and the sovereign: the merchants became "happy taxpayers" and in return the sovereign, with the established army, offered the merchants more stable and bigger market areas, even overseas. As Jan Glete (2002) puts it, a state, in essence, was a military-fiscal establishment. With its remarkably increased power the centralized state was also able to monopolize the use of violence as means of politics. Thus, the organizations—police, gendarme and armed forces—using violence became state monopolies, and so did the production of weapons and gunpowder.

Ancient tribal warfare and warfare prior to establishment of states were, for all practical purposes, symmetric. Fighters of both warring parties were citizen warriors who used the same tactics. For such societies, warfare was an expected part of one's lifestyle. After the establishment of states, such as Sumer or Egypt more than 5,000 years ago, warfare turned one state against another state and an organized army against another organized army. On many occasions the opposing armies were roughly of the same strength, and both sides utilized the same strategies and tactics. Thus, when modern conventional wars began about 500 years ago, they were also symmetric.

Military historian John Keegan (1994) notes that, in the beginning of the nineteenth century, the Prussian war theoretician Karl von Clausewitz recognized as rational and worthwhile "only one form of military organization: the paid and disciplined forces of the bureaucratic state" (p. 245). What Clausewitz did not recognize was the fact that fundamental changes were taking place both in societies and in warfare. Clausewitz himself had fought successfully in the Russian army against Napoleon Bonaparte alongside another type of military organization, the Cossacks. Furthermore, Napoleon himself was not able to face successfully Spanish guerrillas in the Peninsular War (1807–1814) between his forces and the allied powers of Spain, Portugal and Britain. These guerrillas engaged in a different type of warfare. Therefore, we can divide modern warfare into two types: symmetric war between two states, and asymmetric war between a state and a nonstate actor.

During this same period, two political ideologies, nationalism and socialism, helped drive societal change. As Benedict Anderson (1991) described, a nation is an imagined community—a group of people who do not know one another but who nonetheless feel that they belong together. Nationalism refers to such individuals' shared sense of patriotic feeling, principles, or efforts. Socialism started to develop in the nineteenth century as a revolutionary ideology constructed on perceived class differences. Both nationalism and socialism emerged from the French Revolution of 1789 and spread throughout Europe like a bushfire. Nationalism reached Asia toward the end of the nineteenth century and Africa mainly after the First World War.

In ancient tribal societies all men had the obligation to turn into warriors overnight. The French Revolution introduced the same obligation under the title of universal conscription. Every man was a potential fighter and would receive military training. Thus, the idea of warfare and violence as a means of politics changed dramatically. For nonconventional warfare it was highly important that the change blurred the line between soldier and civilian.

Nationalism led to separatism and liberation wars, and revolutionary movements to revolutionary wars, although the two concepts often overlapped, as in the case of the American Revolution of 1776. In such wars, only one party of the struggle was a state with all its resources. This imbalance or asymmetry created the framework for this new type of nonconventional warfare. Karl Marx claimed that in such conflicts the weaker party could survive or defeat the stronger party only by using nonconventional means of warfare.

The theories about and practices of this new type of warfare evolved further in the twentieth century. Vladimir Ilyich Lenin (1906) published an essay titled *Guerrilla Warfare*, in which he stressed the fact that Marxism "does not reject any form of struggle" (p. 213). Lenin was specifically interested in armed struggle conducted by individuals and small groups. For him "a Marxist places himself on the class struggle and not social peace" (p. 213). Although he looked down on the nineteenth-century "Russian terrorists" (it was "an affair of the intellectual conspirator" [p. 214]), he in fact suggested the same tactics: the aim was to assassinate individuals, chiefs and subordinates in the army and police, and to "confiscate monetary funds both from the government and from private persons" (p. 214). Yet, Lenin mentioned some prerequisites: the acts should happen under the strict control of the Social Democratic Labor Party, and they should be carried out at the right time, namely, "when the mass movement has actually reached the point of an uprising" and when "the uprising should assume the higher and more complex form of a prolonged civil war" (p. 216). Finally, warfare should be waged by "the worker combatant" (p. 216).

As Lenin took the baton of nonconventional warfare from Marx, so did Mao Zedong from Lenin. Mao Zedong fully accepted Lenin's suggestion of a prolonged civil war as the framework for guerrilla warfare. For Marx there were three phases in the war: first, the defense against a stronger enemy; second, guerrilla warfare; and third, a popular uprising where the guerrillas go on the offensive and defeat the enemy by means of conventional warfare—a reflection of Karl von Clausewitz's decisive battle.

Mao's main difference between Lenin was his emphasis on the importance of peasant combatants and the control of the countryside; the control of cities would follow almost automatically. Mao's famously said that a guerrilla swims among the people, the villagers in the countryside, like a fish in the sea. Later, Mao's views would be directly reflected in the three-phased war in Vietnam by Vo Nguyen Giap, the commander of Vietminh, League for the Independence of Vietnam, which sought independence for Vietnam from the French. In many cases Giap's "fish" were the villagers. It became very difficult for the enemy to differentiate between a fighter and a civilian. This created a tendency for the French to kill Vietnamese villagers whether they were guerrillas or innocent civilians. The French war efforts in Vietnam came to an end with a crushing defeat in the battle of Dien Bien Phu in 1954.

The United States signed a military and economic aid treaty with South Vietnam in 1961. The United States' involvement in the Vietnam War would peak later, but as early as June 6, 1962, during his speech at the United States Military Academy, President John F. Kennedy presented an accurate picture of the nature of the war the United States was going to face: "We need to be prepared to fight a different war. This is another type of war, new in its intensity, ancient in its origin, war by guerrilla, subversives, insurgents, assassins; war by ambush instead of combat, by infiltration instead of aggression, seeking victory by eroding and exhausting the enemy instead of engaging him and these are the challenges that will be before us in the next decade if freedom is to be saved, a whole new kind of strategy, a wholly different kind of force, and therefore a new and wholly different kind of military training."

A "different kind of war" was also happening during the great wave of decolonization that started with the historical independence of India and Pakistan in 1947 and continued through Asia and Africa in the 1950s and 1960s. The successful liberation organizations had mostly used guerrilla tactics and only rarely committed what might be called terrorist attacks today. It was the guerrillas in the Cuban Revolution who paved the way for the next step in the development of that other kind of nonconventional warfare, terrorism, both in terms of theoretical pondering and Marxist ideological inspiration. The central figures of the Cuban revolution were, for the most part, members of the urban elite: for example, Fidel Castro had studied law, Raul Castro had studied social sciences and Ernesto "Che" Guevara was originally an Argentinean physician. With their urban backgrounds they started to emphasize armed actions in cities. Che Guevara (1961), in his book *La Guerra de Guerillas*, stressed advancing guerrilla operations from urban centers to the countryside. The experiences on the Cuban Sierra Maestra Mountain where the revolutionaries could only survive with the help of the local peasants had taught them a lesson.

Fidel Castro had started a revolution in 1953 to oust President Fulgencio Batista. Soon he was arrested and then released in 1955. He moved to Mexico where he organized a revolutionary group. He landed in Cuba in 1956 with eighty-two fighters, but the troops of Batista either arrested or killed most of them. When Castro was able to escape to Sierra Maestra he had only twelve men left. Above all, they still were guerrillas and referred to their tactics accordingly.

Mirroring ultra-leftist Marxist terrorism, ultra-rightist neo-fascist terrorism also emerged. For example, the members of Nuclei Armati Rivoluzionari, a neo-fascist terrorist organization, killed seventeen people in the so-called Piazza Fontana massacre in Milan, Italy in 1969 and eighty-five persons in a Bologna railway station attack in 1980.

Brazilian Marxist Carlos Marighella published *Minimanual of the Urban Guerilla* in 1969. This publication was meant to be a guide for the struggle against the Brazilian military regime that had come to power in 1964. Marighella defined the urban guerrilla as a person who fights military dictatorship with weapons, using unconventional methods. Such an individual should not appear strange or different from ordinary citizens—Mao's fish swimming in the city. Marighella's objectives were the physical elimination of the leaders of the police and armed forces and the expropriation of government resources, the wealth of rich businessmen and imperialists. The final goal was the creation of a totally new and revolutionary social and political system. Toward this goal, ambushes, bank robberies, executions, explosions, kidnappings, occupations, raids and penetrations should be used. Yet, it is important to note two points. While Marighella was still partly an old-fashioned Maoist-Guevaran guerrilla fighter, the bigger framework for him was that urban guerrillas would only support the emergence and survival of the rural ones, who would have the decisive role in the revolutionary war. He mentioned terrorism in his manual as one of the many "missions" of the urban guerrilla, but for him terrorism was only a technicality, such as using an explosive or firebomb, and not a tactic. In the 1970s a far-left militant group in West Germany, the Baader-Meinhof Group, utilized activities suggested in Marighella's book. The West German government considered this group a terrorist organization.

The urban guerrilla constituted a transitional form of nonconventional warfare between guerrilla and terrorist strategy. Certain factors, such as increased asymmetry between parties in conflict, contributed to this shift. During the decolonization process freedom fighters often had the support of the population both in terms of material and manpower. Consequently, their guerrilla organizations had a reasonable number of boots on the ground. The Cold War also offered them the support of either the Soviet or the Western block, which were testing the other block's strength and readiness to engage in proxy wars. All this started to change with détente, the relaxation of relations between the two superpowers, around 1970.

As governments grew better prepared to fight rebellions in terms of intelligence, police and armed forces, government targets became harder to reach. When the security organizations were better protected, civilian soft targets attracted more attacks.

In 1968 teenagers and students entered a new phase in the twentieth century's so-called youth revolution, which had begun the previous decade with rock music, big American cars, and parties. When Suistola visited several German university campuses in the spring of 1968, these places were literally upside down: the students were aggressively demonstrating and occupying faculty and administrative buildings. As Jerrold Post put it, the goal was "to destroy the world of their fathers" and their acts were "retaliation for real and imagined hurts against the society of their parents" (Post 2015, p. 263). Sometime later the now-iconic pictures of Che Guevara started to appear on the walls of Suistola's fellow students in Finland.

Left-leaning Marxist thinkers, such as Franz Fanon, Antonio Gramsci, Jürgen Habermas and above all Herbert Marcuse, became the "court philosophers" of the radicalized students. Due to the "Marxist awakening" and the disarray of university campuses, a revolutionary situation was created. How to stage the revolution thus became the main question. Some simply resorted to terroristic strategy. The new ultra-leftist Marxists, Trotskyites and Maoists and other similar groups formed only small cell organizations. For example, the infamous Baader-Meinhof Group, throughout its ten-year lifespan, had some sixty to seventy members. And, the majority of them were women. Their enemy was the capitalist society, media and the state, with all its security organizations. They particularly targeted political and business leaders. Ulrike Meinhof (1971) pointed out that the Urban Guerilla Concept—a revolutionary intervention coming from relatively weak revolutionary forces—comes from Latin America. In sum, the rise of terrorism as a strategy was a response to the increasing asymmetry between the warring parties.

The results were striking. In the nineteenth century, the weaker party won a given war only 12 percent of the time, whereas between 1950 and 2000, that figure stood at 55 percent. Why, exactly, have nonconventional warriors been objectively successful in fighting strong conventional armies. To start with, let us consider the question of the economics of warfare. If we were to refer to nonconventional warfare by another name, we might call it "low-cost warfare." As the well-known slogan claims, terrorism is a poor man's weapon. Nonconventional warriors have the ability to cause their enemies high levels of damage at low cost. Compared to conventional armies, guerrilla and terrorist groups are almost always much smaller. Big armed forces need extensive communication systems to fight in a coordinated way, and often they use very expensive military hardware, whereas the other party uses Kalashnikovs and low-tech bombs. Put simply, big is expensive, and small is cheap. And as a result, the training to become a guerrilla or terrorist fighter is also short and cheap.

Modern armed forces also need a huge number of support troops: for example, to keep one soldier fighting on the front line in Vietnam, there had to be fourteen other people supporting him. The cost per soldier per year for the U.S. Armed Forces in Iraq in 2008 was $4 million and in Afghanistan in 2011, $2.5 million (Belasco 2014). The cost to kill one Taliban fighter has been estimated to be around $50 million. It is difficult to present the exact financial circumstances of U.S. enemies, but when Pakistan's Inter-Services Intelligence (ISI) supported the Taliban in Afghanistan, the calculated per-troop cost for ISI was about $1,200 (Gall 2013).

A guerrilla and terrorist organization can also use certain "financing methods" that a state cannot use. Carlos Marighella (1969) suggested that one such method was bank robbery and another one was the expropriation of government resources and the wealth of rich businessmen and landowners. Such methods also include kidnappings and ransoms, drug trafficking and lately, in the case of ISIS, trading oil and antiquities. According to UN calculations, ISIS earned $35–$45 million between November 2013 and October 2014 from ransoms. The Security Institute at University of Exeter estimated that during the first five months of 2015 ISIS had collected over $100 million from the antiquity business.

Guerrilla and terrorist groups typically begin as small cell organizations, and their members are often only part-time guerrillas or terrorists who have ordinary jobs with salaries (Marighella 1969). Thus, the financial obligations of a cell organization are very low. If the group grows bigger and more settled, the expenses start to increase. That happens especially when the organization gains control over a certain territory. In such a case it has to take on the burden of running at least some functions of a state, such as taking care of social security, health care and education. On the other hand, such functions help the organization to rally popular and financial support and to boost group cohesion.

The low financial cost of terrorist activities makes it easy to spread terrorism. The cost of organizing the September 11, 2001 attacks was about $500,000. The ISIS attack in Paris in November 2015 cost only about $12,000. The money needed to kidnap a journalist or aid worker and behead them before a camera is likely even cheaper, but the horrible impact of such acts can be enormous and have global ramifications.

Guerilla and terrorist organizations have one other strategic advantage in pursuit of their ends: the willingness of their members to kill—and die—for their cause. This form of "altruism" communicates a firm trust that one is fighting for a higher and more important aim—be it the Marxist Revolution, the liberation of one's people or the formation of a self-declared Caliphate. Altruism within an organization, on a more general level, is also considered a necessity for people's tolerance for high numbers of casualties, for group cohesion and for trust among group members.

2

LARGE-GROUP IDENTITY AND PREJUDICE

Psychoanalytic Perspectives

Questions of identity—"Who are we, and who is the Other?"—are key factors in moderating in-group altruism and out-group aggression. How individuals and groups respond to such questions, whether consciously or unconsciously, affect how they relate to one another and to the Other—and determine when the killing of the Other is considered not only permissible but also mandatory. This feature of the human condition may be universal under the right circumstances, but its roots are perhaps less clear. Indeed, are humans wired to kill or do we learn to kill? The answer is not one of either nature or nurture, but both.

A very simplified version of the evolutionary perspective claims that human brains have become wired to kill as a response to Darwinian survival struggle. As a result, the fittest—the most aggressive human—has survived by having the ability to kill. The survival of the fittest theory has a recent competitor, "the survival of the fattest" theory. Survival of the fittest often relies on only one sustenance method, whereas according to survival of the fattest, a person who puts his or her eggs into several baskets accumulates sizeable energy reserves in the body. Consequently, the fattest person is more flexible in adapting to environmental changes with alternative survival strategies, and might have survived because of his or her ability to feed our most energy consuming organ, the brain, thus making the brain's growth possible (Wrangham 2009).

Most animals kill only for subsistence. Like humans, our closest relatives, chimpanzees, also kill for other reasons. Chimpanzees can stage raids and even genocides (Goodall 2010). A peaceful human past is an urban myth. About 90–95 percent of all human societies have waged wars. Between 800,000 years ago and the Neolithic Age, which started about 12,500 years ago, there are at least ten different cases of documented intra- or intergroup cannibalism. Archeologists and historians have documented mass murders as well. For example, there are fifty-nine buried persons in a 12,000–14,000-year-old cemetery in Nubia, a region along the Nile River, and there are clear signs that over 40 percent of them had been killed either with a lance or arrow. At Crow Creek, South Dakota, an archeologist found a mass grave of over 500 people slaughtered and mutilated about 700 years ago. Prehistoric tribal warfare was more lethal than we can imagine (Keeley 1996).

If killing serves human survival, how exactly does it do so? American archeologist Steve A. LeBlanc states that killing deals with resource stress; often we are short of certain things and try to solve problems by violent means—by conquest, plunder and elimination of rivals. The main "commodities" for which we kill others are food and, for males (as for male chimpanzees, too), females (LeBlanc and Register 2003). Cognitive psychologist Steven Pinker (2011) offers a more detailed list of things we kill for. He starts with LeBlanc's "solutions" for resource stress and then adds the wish to dominate and take revenge and also to support an ideology.

Richard Ned Lebow (2010), a political scientist, analyzed ninety-four large-scale conflicts after the 1648 Peace Treaty of Westphalia that ended the Thirty Years' War in Europe and established the balance of power system in international relations. According to Lebow's statistics, the dignity or honor of a state was the reason for war in 58 percent of the cases, whereas revenge motivated 10 percent. Issues arising from resource stress or from a drive for material benefits constituted the principle reason in only 7 percent of the cases. Moreover, Lebow claimed that in almost all of those wars the initiator also lost the war and that, in the present international system, war and territorial conquest are counterproductive. It is important to note that Lebow was referring only to state-level actors and, to a large extent, great powers and that, for 150 years after the treaty, absolutism was the prevailing form of government. Thus, kings or emperors decided what the state's interests were and when to go to war.

Recently, some research has been done to find an interplay between brain and politics, with an aim to explain human nature and especially mass political orientation, wars and other aggressive human interactions (Fowler and Darren 2008; Jost, Nam, Amodio, and van Bavel 2014; Vander Valk 2012). Whether scientists in this burgeoning field of "political neuroscience" will be able to come up with data that can be useful in observing and dealing with human behaviour and that can be applied to understanding international affairs remains to be seen.

Psychoanalysts have also considered human evolution in speculating about why humans kill the Other. For example, Erik Erikson (1966) used the term *pseudo species* in describing the evolution of humans into groups such as tribes and clans. He added that groups then behaved "as if they were separate species, created at the beginning of time by supernatural intent" (p. 606). He went on to speculate further about group formation among primitive humans. He theorized that primitive people sought a measure of protection for their unbearable nakedness by adopting the armor of the lower animals and wearing their skins, feathers or claws. On the basis of these outer garments, each tribe, clan, or group evolved a sense of shared identity. Furthermore, Erikson stated that each group feared the human who belonged to another subspecies of humankind, and each group developed "*a distinct sense of identity,* but also a conviction of harboring *the* human identity" (p. 606). This attitude fortified each pseudo species by engendering the belief that the others were "extraspecific and inimical to 'genuine' human endeavor" (p. 606).

Vamık Volkan (2013) attempted to expand Erikson's supposition, also speculative, that may further explain what happened during the course of human evolution. For centuries, neighboring tribes, due to their natural boundaries, had only each other to interact with. Neighboring groups had to compete for territory, food, sex and physical goods for their survival. Eventually, this primitive level of competition assumed more psychological implications. Physical essentials, besides retaining their status as genuine necessities, absorbed mental meanings. Prestige, honor, power, envy, revenge, humiliation, loss and submission evolved from being tokens of survival to becoming large-group symbols, cultural amplifiers, traditions, religions or historical memories that embedded a large group's self-esteem, narcissism and identity.

Erikson's postulations are supported by references to the Other in many ancient documents and languages. Ancient Chinese regarded themselves as *people* and viewed the Other as *kuei* or "hunting spirits." The Apache Indians considered themselves to be *indeh*, the people, and all others as *indah*, the enemy (Boyer 1986). The Mundurucu in the Brazilian rain forest divided their world into Mundurucu, who were people, and non-Mundurucu, who were *pariwat* (enemies), except for certain friendly neighbors (Murphy 1957). There are other examples of large groups who consider only themselves as "people," such as the Sudanese Dinka (the name of the group translates as "people") and Nuer ("original people"), and the Arctic Yupiks ("real people") (Harari 2014). Anthropologist Howard Stein stated that this type of pattern "cannot be literally generalized to all cultures, but it shows in the extreme a universal proclivity in feelings towards, perception of, and action taken against those who were not 'the' people" (Stein 1990, p. 118). During the times about which written history is available we constantly see examples of one group seeing the other as less than human in interactions demonstrating Erikson's *pseudo species* concept. One of the best-known examples is the distinction the ancient Greeks made between themselves as civilized people and "barbarians," such as the Persians. The term "barbarians" even indicates that they were not able to speak a proper language, and thus, they were barbarians, the "mumblers." The Christian Europeans' treatment of Jews during the Middle Ages (and in much more recent centuries), the white Americans' treatment of Native and African Americans in the United States, the Nazis' behavior and much more recent crimes against humanity such as witnessed in the former Yugoslavia, Rwanda and Syria are examples of one large group dehumanizing another.

Here, the term "large group" indicates those who share a sense of sameness—tribal, ethnic, national, religious or ideological—and of belonging. This belonging extends beyond subgroupings of family, professional, social and gender identifications, and may consist of tens, hundreds or thousands of people who may never come in personal contact with one another. Such identification with a large group is a very natural human phenomenon, one that provides self-esteem, pride and pleasure for its members. Yet, it has a downside as well: shared prejudice. Our discussion will not focus on dichotomies such as female/male, gay/straight, rich/poor, educated/not educated, but rather on shared large-group prejudices toward other large groups. Shared prejudice of this kind, when revealed, can become malignant and articulated in terms of "us versus them," focusing only on differences rooted in various historical and geographical events. Consider these terms: *racism, neo-racism, apartheid, ethnic hatred, fascism, xenophobia, anti-Semitism, Islamophobia, anti-Westernization,* and *national exceptionalism* and *extreme religious fundamentalism.* These all-too-familiar words and the distinctions they make are necessary in order to clarify situations as they exist in today's changing world.

A most common type of prejudice shared by one large group toward another is racism, and whether recognized or denied, it has been, and is, a defining element of human experience. Justification for racism and racial discrimination was traditionally built on a pseudo-scientific thesis that proclaims that the races are unequal, and the "lower" races are "deficient" in personality, intellect and culture. Modern racist theories—neo-racism in Europe—expand prejudice to encompass wider, more anthropological bases such as family structure, social value systems, language and religion as justification for segregating communities. When shared prejudice about the Other becomes malignant, humans justify humiliating and killing them.

In order to understand prejudice as it is shared by large groups, we must first define what large-group identity is and how it comes into being. Although occasionally adults adopt a large-group identity, such as when an adult joins a new group such as ISIS, one's identity usually begins in childhood. From infancy on, children are exposed to common elements that have evolved through both myths and the realities of historical beginnings and geographical realities that span linguistic, cultural, religious and ideological realms. They grow up hearing terms of commonality: We are Danes. We are Romany. We are Christians. We are Socialists—and/or You are Pakistani. You are Chinese. You are Muslim. You are a capitalist.

The *subjective experience* of individual identity that evolves from childhood is defined as a persistent sense of sameness within oneself, even while sharing characteristics with others (Erikson 1956). Adults often use many labels simultaneously to define their social or professional identity— parent, carpenter, musician or soccer player. These terms explain individual identity on a somewhat surface level, and are therefore not the same as a person's experience of sustained sameness and inner solidity that come from early belonging to a large group (Akhtar 1999b; Volkan 1997, 2013, 2014c).

The mind of the human infant is remarkably and surprisingly active, as scientific studies of recent decades have shown (Stern 1985; Emde 1991; Lehtonen 2003; Bloom 2010). There is a psychobiological potential of we-ness and bias toward one's own kind even in the early months and years, as the infant or small child experiences a restricted small group of family and caregivers. This sense of we-ness is limited, however, since the child is yet incapable of embracing the emotional or intellectual dimensions of more expansive large-group identity concepts such as nationality, ethnicity, tribal affiliation, religion, or political ideology. Infants and small children are *generalists* (Erikson 1956) when it comes to these affiliations, and it is only later in childhood that the subjective experience and intellectual knowledge of belonging to a large group develops.

As summarized by Finish psychoanalyst and researcher Johannes Lehtonen (2016), the newborn's sudden entry into extra-uterine life is profound and entirely new, as they must suddenly initiate breathing and sucking to sustain themselves and are stimulated by senses of taste, smell and hearing, as well as movement and thumb sucking. Lehtonen references clinical observations and research (Cheour et al. 2002; Denton, McKinley, Farrell, and Egan 2009; Hofer 2014; Kandel 2006; Lappi et al. 2007; Purhonen et al. 2005) that explore the bond between mother or mothering adult and the child. This merger between infant and caretaker builds a soothing and life-supporting internal image within the infant to which sensations coming from inside the infant contribute. Observations of the smiling and vocal responses of two- to three-month-old infants reveal that they develop internal images of others, even though such images are not yet stabilized or differentiated from other such images (Fonagy 2001; Salonen

1989; Spitz, 1965; Tyson and Tyson 1990; Winnicott 1963). Theoretically, we surmise that the concept of the Other emerges at this time, a necessary development for the infant's mind and adaptation to life. Bad experiences with these early attachments may later become subject matter for the psychoanalyst's couch (Fonagy 2001; Volkan and Akhtar 1997).

As time passes, children begin to separate their own mental images from those of others, integrating different aspects of both types of images (Mahler 1968; Kernberg 1976; Volkan 1976). They identify with a range of aspects of important individuals in their environment from realistic ones to fantasized, wished for, and even frightening ones. They absorb mothering, fathering, sibling, and other mentoring functions and psychological ways of handling life's problems. These identifications with those in close relationship to them also embrace concrete and abstract large-group identity markers such as language, nursery rhymes and songs, cultural traditions and symbols, myths and religious beliefs and rituals and images of their history, including heroes, martyrs and significant events. Through these things children expand their internal world to relate first to their own small group and as they grow older, to the larger group to which they belong. Freud (1939) noted that parents represent the greater society to their child. This, of course, includes identification with their parents' and other important persons' prejudices.

A related concept is what is known in psychoanalysis as *individuation*. As children develop mentally they go through a process in which they "separate and individuate" themselves from mother and other caregivers, in a sense psychologically pushing them away (Mahler 1968). Through childhood and as adults we all internally define ourselves through other people. In addition to identifications we readily recognize as ours, we consciously or unconsciously compare ourselves to others, in admiration or envy, inspiration or competition. Important people close to us—family members, friends, professional associates—are parts of us on an unconscious level, negatively or positively, and we identify with them because we use them as temporary or more permanent reservoirs of our unwanted but sometimes wished-for self-images. As we choose our proximity to them—drawing closer or avoiding them—we remain connected to life with all its experiences, desires, fantasies and shared prejudices. As children grow and their concept of Other expands beyond mother and those in their immediate circle of experience, they can now define the Other using criteria from a larger societal perspective: a large group of people who do not belong to the child's own sense of we-ness.

A concept that closely resembles identification is *depositing* (Volkan, Ast, and Greer 2002; Volkan 2013, 2014c). In contrast to identification in which children are the primary actors in collecting images, perceptions and tasks from their environment and experiences and making them their own, in depositing it is an adult in the child's life who feels the need to put something—an image connected with specific psychological tasks—into the child's psyche. The *replacement child* is a well-known example of this concept (Poznanski 1972; Cain and Cain 1964; Volkan and Ast 1997). If a mother's first child dies and she delivers a second child, she relates to the new child, mostly without being aware of it, as if the new child is the first child. The replacement child is sometimes given the name of the child that died, put in that child's bed, and is given the dead child's toys. Since the new child has no experience of the dead one, it is the mother (or mothering person) who gives her new child the image of the dead child and tasks the new child to keep the dead child "alive." Replacement children adjust to this psychological situation in various ways according to genetic and environmental factors.

Adults who experience severe trauma during which their large group is threatened, such as during war or other situations, may also deposit their traumatized self-image into the developing identities of their children. Volkan closely studied the life of an analysand who as a child was a reservoir for the extremely traumatized image of his father figure, a survivor of a Japanese prison camp and the Bataan Death March in the Philippines. The father figure was severely traumatized because of his American large-group identity by people who, as they were Japanese, had a different large-group identity. This child grew up to become a sadistic animal killer because the task deposited in him was to be a hunter instead of being the hunted one like his father figure had been during the war (Volkan 2014a). Psychoanalytic literature provides many examples of Holocaust survivors who passed images and tasks to their offspring and the various ways these offspring psychologically responded to such transgenerational transmissions in ways that range from creative to troublesome (Brenner 2014; Fromm 2011; Volkan, Ast, and Greer 2002). As reservoirs for deposited images and tasks passed down to them to deal with these images, these children psychologically become links in their family history, sometimes over generations, especially when their ancestors' large-group histories involve trauma.

Descendants of victimizers too may experience similar processes, including severe difficulty or inability to mourn (Mitscherlich and Mitscherlich 1975; Volkan 2013, 2014c). Perpetrators' descendants are more preoccupied with shared feelings of guilt and their consequences than with shared feelings of victimization and helplessness. One analysand, a German man, had a symptom since he was an adolescent: he "sleepwalked" and tried to smash his bedroom windows, sometimes succeeding. As an adult, success at work made him feel guilty. During analysis he was able to recognize that his grandfather had been an important Nazi figure involved in gassing "unwanted" persons when they were locked in a bus. Before this, he thought his grandfather had been a hero who was killed during the war. Analytic work helped him disown the image of his grandfather that had been deposited into him by his parents and helped him understand that his symptom of breaking windows—like one of his grandfather's victims in a locked bus—was an expression of guilt. Afterward, he began having a more comfortable life and he became a businessman. Through utilizing sublimation he cultivated certain types of trees that increase oxygen in the air, reversing his grandfather's task and ridding himself of guilt (Volkan 2015).

We have described a kind of "psychological DNA" that is created within the child that becomes a foundation for his or her identity formation. Anne Ancelin Schützenberger's "ancestor syndrome" (1998), Judith Kestenberg's term "transgenerational transportation" (1982), and Haydée Faimberg's description of the "telescoping of generations" (2005) refer to depositing traumatized images.

Depositing in *large-group psychology*, which also starts in childhood, is shared by tens, hundreds of thousands or millions of people and becomes "*shared* psychological DNA," creating a sense of belonging. A collective catastrophe inflicted by an enemy group affects people individually, but they are left with self-images similarly (though not identically) traumatized by the massive event. These many individuals deposit such images into their children and give them tasks such as: "Regain my self-esteem for me," "Put my mourning process on the right track," "Be assertive and take revenge," or "Never forget and remain alert."

Though each child in the second generation owns an individual identity, all share similar links to the same massive trauma's image and similar unconscious tasks for coping with it. Since the next generation will probably not be successful in fulfilling their shared tasks, they will pass them along to the third generation, and so on. Such conditions create a powerful unseen network among thousands, sometimes millions of people.

Through the years all the people in the large group remain linked to the past with the mental images of the ancestors' historical event, complete with heroes, martyrs, victimization and other feelings. The meaning of the tasks for new generations goes through what psychoanalysts call "change of function" (Waelder 1930) in which the mental image of the event becomes a significant large-group identity marker, a "chosen trauma" (Volkan 1991, 2006, 2013, 2014c). This term is not meant to imply that the large group "chooses" to be victimized by another large group and subsequently lose self-esteem. It does, however, recognize that the group "chooses" to psychologize and dwell on a past traumatic event and make it a major large-group identity marker. There are many historic examples that illustrate this: Serbians hold the image of the 1389 Battle of Kosovo; for Greeks it is the image of the fall of Constantinople in the year 1453; Scots revere the 1746 Battle of Culloden; and Dakota Indians hold the image of the 1890 battle of Wounded Knee. For Jewish persons the Holocaust has become a most significant large-group marker, even though Orthodox Jews still refer to the 586 BC destruction of the Jewish temple in Jerusalem by Nebuchadnezzar II of Babylonia as the trauma linking all Jewish people. These kinds of transgenerational conveyances of long-term "tasks" perpetuate the cycle of societal trauma and shared prejudice toward the Other as a large group.

Another key concept for the evolution of large-group identity is *suitable targets of externalization*. Again we return to the development of the young child: at about eight months of age infants recognize that not all the faces around them belong to their caregivers, known in psychoanalysis as *stranger anxiety* (Spitz 1965; Parens 1979). This normal phenomenon marks the infant's recognition of the unfamiliar Other, the stranger, and is the source for future "normal" prejudice. Children begin to notice that not everything in their world belongs to their large group; there are strangers also belonging to a large group. Children learn about *shared targets*, mostly inanimate things, from adults around them, and through them they learn *experientially* what belongs to their large group and what does not (Volkan 2013, 2014c).

A good example of this concept can be found in Vamık Volkan's birthplace, Cyprus, where Greeks and Turks have been physically divided into two separate communities since 1974, having previously lived together for centuries. As pork is part of the Greek diet, Greek farmers often raise pigs. While all children love farm animals, a Turkish child would be discouraged from touching a piglet, however adorable, as it would be perceived as "dirty," because Muslim Turks do not eat pork. Pigs do not belong in the Turk's large group, and for the Turkish child the pig will be regarded as a cultural amplifier for the Greeks. In a concrete sense what is externalized into the image of the pig will not be reinternalized, will not be "eaten" psychologically. For the Turkish child, the pig has become a reservoir for externalizing *permanently* his or her "unwanted" parts. Let us explain what we mean by "unwanted parts." Infants and small children have mixed experiences, both loving and frustrating, when relating to their mother and other caregivers, including "good" feeding and "bad" feeding experiences (Stern 1985). Small children need to integrate their "loved" and "unloved" parts and correspondingly "loving" and "frustrating" images of mother and others. Unintegrated "bad" aspects of the self and caretakers remain in their minds as "unwanted" elements.

The small Turkish child does not fully understand what Greekness means when experiencing a piglet as a target of externalization. It will take some time for sophisticated thoughts and perceptions associated with emotions and historic knowledge about the Other as a large group to evolve. The child will not be aware that the symbol of the Other originally was in the service of helping the child avoid feeling tensions due to keeping unwanted parts within. When the child finds a suitable target for "unwanted parts," the precursor of the unfamiliar Other as a large group becomes established in the child's mind at an experimental level (Volkan 1988). In this book when we use the term "Other" we will refer only to unfamiliar large groups, ethnic, national, ideological and religious large groups to which we do not belong.

Living in America, far from Old World anti-Semitism, some Jewish children of Polish origin were taught to spit three times when passing a Catholic Church (Itzkowitz 2000). Although it may have been superstition, it also personifies the notion of the church as a suitable target of externalization. Even in an atmosphere of comparative safety, memories of "bad" targets of externalization linger. Except for those who were brought as slaves, people of different nationalities and religions came to the United States with a vision of an idealized American large-group identity. Even so, this vision has not always been shared by all inhabitants of the United States. Because of the shared idealized American large-group identity, the suitable target of externalization to which historian Norman Itzkowitz referred might not be as stable as the suitable target is for the Turkish child in Cyprus.

Unintegrated "good" images also find suitable targets of permanent externalization that, as the child grows, represent "we-ness" and become significant large-group identity markers. For example, Finnish children use the sauna for their "good" reservoir. Only when Finnish children grow up will they have sophisticated thoughts and feelings about Finnishness. Not only do children possess certain cultural amplifiers, such as language, nursery rhymes, food, dances, and religious symbols, but they also make these amplifiers "good" targets of permanent externalization.

Historical events with emotional import may increase a large group's investment in its own target of externalization. A very recognizable example of such a symbol is the Scottish kilt that dates from the thirteenth century. It was an event in the eighteenth century however that transformed the tartan kilt into a shared "good" reservoir of Scottishness. With the defeat of Bonnie Prince Charles at Culloden in 1746, the English banned the wearing of the kilt in Scotland under the Act of Proscription. The act was repealed thirty-six years later, and the kilt was adopted as Scottish military dress. King George IV made a state visit to Scotland in 1882, strengthening the Scottish investment in the kilt, which served to enhance Scottish "we-ness" in the face of a visit from the figurehead of powerful England. Many Scottish families even today have and wear their own tartan design, and the dress continues to serve as an ethnic reservoir signifying Scottishness.

In addition to their own personal identities, tens, hundreds of thousands or millions of children utilize the same suitable targets to externalize their unwanted or idealized parts, thereby maintaining and contributing to the evolution of large-group identities. The Other as another large group can become a target of shared prejudice, in varying degrees and according to external circumstances. To illustrate benign, hostile or malignant consequences of shared prejudice by large groups, Volkan came up with the metaphor of a tent (Volkan 1988, 1997, 2006). Picture two fabric-like layers that we learn to wear from childhood. The first layer, the individual one, fits each of us snugly, like clothing. This is one's core personal identity that provides an inner sense of persistent sameness. The second layer is like a tent canvas, loose fitting, but allowing a huge number of individuals to share a sense of sameness with each other under the same large-group enclosure. Large-group identity markers appear as colorful designs stitched on the canvas of each large group's metaphorical tent.

There are subgroups and subgroup identities under the huge large-group tent, such as professional and political identities. The tent pole, representing the political leader and the governing body, holds the tent erect (Volkan and Fowler 2009), but it is the tent's canvas that psychologically protects those inside, including the leader, other persons with authority, and all members of the large group. Although there may be dissenters in a large group, they do not change the essential shared sentiments within the large group unless they develop a sizeable number of followers, such as those in terrorist organizations who become a political force, an important subgroup or even a different type of large group such as ISIS. From the view of individual psychology, a person may perceive the tent pole as a father figure (Freud 1921) and the canvas as a nurturing mother (Kernberg 1980; Anzieu 1984; Chasseguet-Smirgel 1984). From a large-group psychology point of view the canvas represents the psychological border of large-group identity that is shared by tens, hundreds of thousands or millions of people (Volkan 2013, 2014c)

In recent years an unprecedented surge of migrants and refugees have flooded into Europe. They represent the Other who are threatening the stability of the psychological borders of the host countries. Many individuals in these countries are terrified that their country's social customs, security and economics will be damaged and that they will not be able to support a massive influx of newcomers. Terrorist attacks took place in November 2015 in Paris and in March 2016 in Brussels, increasing national security concerns. Even in the United States many governors openly declared that they would not allow Syrian refugees to settle in their states. U.S. President Donald Trump spoke openly during his 2016 presidential campaign about banning Muslims who are not American citizens from entering the United States at all. When there is a flood of immigrants, refugees and asylum seekers the host country's population usually becomes divided into two sections. Those who are able to keep their individual identities independent of the impact of large-group sentiments become willing to open the tent's gate and accept the huge number of newcomers. Those who perceive the newcomers as opening holes in, and thus damaging, the metaphorical large-group tent's canvas—the border of large-group identity—become anxious and defensively perceive the huge immigrant population as a threat. They may develop hostile, even malignant shared prejudice. Polarization in the host country can lead to new political and social concerns and complications, especially when some politicians use shared feelings of fear or disgust to promote their own political agenda (Volkan 2017).

Now let us imagine two huge large-group tents standing side by side. The canvas of each tent provides both a physical and a *psychological border* for each large group. The nature of shared prejudice between the two large groups can be visualized as that which members under one tent throw at the canvas of the adjacent tent. It may range from mud that can be washed away, to filthy waste material that sticks, to bullets that kill. Individuals alone and, in wars and warlike situations, together express their *aggression* in its malignant form toward the Other.

Since Sigmund Freud's (1930) declaration that aggression is an innate, instinctual and independent disposition of humanity, psychoanalysts have tended to interpret the psychological reasons for every war in the light of this basic idea. Although it is an inescapable observation that the human race is endowed with aggression, psychoanalysts, in general, for a long time did not study the many ways in which facets of this instinctual drive interact with other issues in the genesis of war. The pessimism Freud (1932) expressed in his reply to Albert Einstein's plea that Freud find a solution for humanity's proclivity for armed conflict set up a model for his followers and encouraged them to leave political matters, including declarations and conduct of war, to statesmen. His assertion in his reply to Einstein that it was not profitable to consult an "unworldly theoretician" on such an urgent human problem went unchallenged. Earlier Freud (1915) had noted the disillusionment about civilized values that war brings by its return to barbarism, which is ever resurgent in wartime. Nevertheless, psychoanalyst Jacob Arlow (1973) suggested that perhaps Freud was more optimistic than he appeared, since Freud considered the "cultural process" to be biologically determined. It was Freud's view that as individual development moves toward the ego's reliable mastery of instinctual drives, so does cultural evolution move to strengthen the intellect and the internalization and taming of aggressive impulses. This hoped-for transformation has obviously not as yet taken place.

Reviewing psychoanalytic formulations about war, Vamık Volkan (1979) joined Alexander Mitscherlich (1971) in suggesting that psychoanalytic research on the collective aggression of large groups must not be dismissed from consideration; investigation of the psychology of war should not exclude those who are experts in clinical psychological issues and psychological theories. Psychoanalysts should not restrict themselves to a medical or clinical position; an interdisciplinary approach is clearly indicated. Volkan suggested further that wars should be considered one by one, since, like patients, they may have many apparent similarities but be different from one another in highly significant ways. Such a case-by-case approach is recommended as an aid to understanding not only the psychological determinants of any given war but also its impact on the people involved in it.

Long ago Edward Glover (1933), although referring to war as "mass insanity," saw it also as containing a "curative process," holding that just as insanity is itself a dramatic attempt to deal with conflict on the level of the individual, war is an attempt on the collective level to cure some disharmony, however doomed it may be to result in hopeless disintegration. The notion of war as "therapy" can be found in other writings also (Fornari 1966; Mitscherlich 1971).

Patriotism too has a positive aspect of exalting a group through acceptable and legitimate channels, serving as a displacement of an individual's narcissism, and it can also engage the projected hate component of ambivalence. Societies accept having war institutions and, at certain times, preparations for engaging in a war (Atkin 1971), although every scenario is different. At any rate, there is merit in studying and clinically observing any group's reactions to war and their processes involved in it, so we might expand our understanding of group conflict in general.

According to Edward Glover (1933), civilized nations are disadvantaged in war because they lack the ritual element of control in killing that primitive people have, and they don't understand the "purity" of punishing rage toward the enemy. Modern wars, like all wars, bring elements of misery beyond armed conflict alone, including imprisonment, discrimination and invasive change that affect all of society. When we consider today's violent confrontations, with our new methods of killing and terrorizing the Other—the main topic of this book—we must think beyond the battlefield to consider all kinds of persecution and their potential ramifications, including fear and loss, of people, places and life as they know it.

At the present time a deep interest in wars and especially terrorism is evolving within psychoanalytic circles. Today's psychoanalytic literature finds little use for psychoanalytic theories on aggression that go all the way back to Sigmund Freud's various thoughts on this topic before 1920, followed by his ideas about the "death instinct" (Freud 1920). Most considerations on aggression now fit into Henri Parens' (1979) "multi-trends theory of aggression." Parens states that the way parents rear their child is a direct factor in that child's aggression profile, while he also considers the role played by a child's average-expectable biological conditions in this profile. The quality of attachment to important others in a child's environment and the child's aggression profile are linked. Parens describes a wide range of expressions of aggression, from anger to hostility, to rage, to hate, to malignant prejudice.

There are various factors that turn shared prejudice to hostility, malignant acts, wars, guerrilla activities and terrorism. Such factors to which we will refer later include the personality organization of a political leader or a leader of a guerrilla or terrorist organization. For example, some leaders who possess a narcissistic personality organization may perceive a special Other as representing a threat to their grandiose self (Post 2015; Volkan 2004, 2009; Wirth 2009). They then manipulate politics to turn their followers' shared prejudice into a hostile or malignant one against this specific Other. Like Adolf Hitler, they may even initiate genocidal events to purify themselves from the "unwanted" Other (Volkan and Fowler 2009). Often the image of ancestor's trauma at the hand of the Other who had become a historical large-group identity marker is reactivated and becomes connected with an ideology providing a sense of entitlement for the large group: to recover what was lost in reality and fantasy during the collective trauma that evolved into what Volkan called a *chosen trauma* (Volkan 1991, 2013, 2014c). This creates a *time collapse*: shared anxieties, expectations, fantasies, and defenses associated with the past magnify the image of current conflicts. Large groups become psychologically willing to engage in more hostile or malignant prejudice, sadistic or masochistic acts, and perpetrate monstrous cruelty against the Other.

In addition to those groups to which people are born, people can be attracted to and become members of other types of large group *as adults*. Religious cults, guerrilla movements and terrorist organizations such as the Branch Davidians, Fuerzas Armadas Revolucionarias de Colombia (FARC; the Revolutionary Armed Forces of Colombia) and ISIS illustrate the formation of the second type of large group.

Members of such organizations and lone wolves attached to terrorist organizations function under the dominant impact of this second type of large-group identity. Individuals in a crowd intensively protesting or supporting a cause or even a sports team may lose their individuality, but this loss is temporary. Members of terrorist organization lose not only their individual identities but also their old beliefs, moral attitudes and even behavior patterns. For them, this development is not temporary. This phenomenon helps explain why mass suicides sometimes occur in religious cults.

Similarly, terrorists or suicide bombers do not perform inhumane acts simply because of problems stemming from their individual identities in childhood or because of morals and behaviors learned in childhood. Often, they perform them despite their childhood identity and sense of morality. They perceive their horrible acts as a sacred duty, a necessary act to protect or bring attention to their adopted large-group identity. Such large-groups are typically mission based—whether religious, ideological or terroristic.

Volkan studied the lives of David Koresh (born Vernon Wayne Howell), who would become the cult leader of the Branch Davidians at Waco, Texas, and Osama bin Laden, who would become the leader of al-Qaeda (Volkan 2013). He concluded that their traumatic childhoods played the key role in their search to be the leader of a "new family" (a cult and a terrorist organization, respectively) with a mission to reverse or deny old humiliations. Individuals needing to find a container to maintain or raise their self-esteem become members of these types of groups and join their mission. For terrorist large groups nothing seems to appeal more strongly or successfully than the possibility of taking part in "success" itself, even in a social matrix in which shame, guilt and empathy vanish.

3

JUSTIFICATIONS FOR KILLING THE OTHER

People have found justification for killing humans belonging to the opposing large group in a conflict since ancient times, and attempts to look at killing the Other from a conceptualized perspective have existed since early Greek philosophers' contributions. Characterization of war against barbarians as a natural, just action appears in Plato's *Politics*. Plato compares war to hunting, especially if it is waged against people who should be "destined by nature to be governed, but will not submit" (Nussbaum 1943, p. 453). However, from the time of the Peloponnesian War of Thucydides, during which utmost cruelty was exhibited, Greeks had certain rules to follow during wartime; even then there was a kind of *jus in bello*, law in waging war. Out of respect for each other, one of the usual practices was to allow both sides a time to make animal offerings to the Gods before a battle. The aim of this practice was not only to ask for luck in the battle, but also for permission to kill humans.

The Roman orator and philosopher Marcus Tullius Cicero considered and described areas where there would be a departure from justifying war. For Cicero, the right state for humans was peace. He stressed the fact that war should serve good purposes. As a result, a Roman ruler should have a just cause for war—self-defense, reaction to an earlier evil and, interestingly, religion, to fight for the Gods. Cicero also stressed the peaceful way of settling issues through discussion rather than force. For him, the former was appropriate for human beings, the latter for beasts.

St. Augustine of Hippo (ca. 354–430) became a most influential figure in crystallizing the *just-war* concept. He accomplished this by establishing a balance between two realms: God and the Emperor. He concluded that a Christian can serve both. To serve the Emperor meant above all to serve in the army and kill people. A Christian should also follow the Fifth Commandment: "Thou shalt not kill." St. Augustine outlined conditions when killing was acceptable. Following Cicero's ideas he accepted self-defense and compensation for a past evil as causes for just war. In a way, he also adapted Cicero's third just cause, religion, although with a difference. He applied the principle to the structure of Christian faith and ended up with the view that a just war could also be waged to punish a sinner for betraying a moral principle. Thus, St. Augustine expanded the understanding of waging war by linking it to a divine purpose to further the will of God and the teachings of the Bible (Delahunty and Yoo 2012).

Now the following problem had to be faced: If one submits to the idea that there is a moral code granting permission to kill on just grounds and even to kill to defend that moral code, there is no end to such violence. Other sets of norms had to be followed to tackle this problem. As a result, a competition among those ideas and their supporters evolved. Each party began to claim that their own set of ideas was the correct one. This encouraged the new organizations to generate their own sets of conditions for just action, as a terrorist organization does. Diana Francis (2004) observed that just causes have been expanded to cover wars to oust dictators and oppressive governments and to stop those carrying out military invasions or perpetrating genocide. If St. Augustine were to return to life, he would likely be greatly surprised by how his original doctrine has been interpreted.

While the idea of just war had a religious connotation, it also invited the development of earthly ideologies. The political ideologies and political parties in a modern sense began to emerge with the French Enlightenment in the eighteenth century. Individuals who were not officially connected with running the state began to involve themselves in societal matters.

Political ideologies began to offer explanations for what was wrong in contemporary society, how the right conditions should be constructed, how to recognize obstacles and enemies and how to eliminate enemies. In the eighteenth century the remains of the medieval feudal society were still in place and the political power was in the hands of the absolute king and his court. Hence, power was not based on knowledge or education, but on heritage, and the people with education (such as educators and administrators) and sometimes even those with money (such as merchants) had little or no power.

Philosophers such as Jean-Jacques Rousseau and Voltaire were able to recognize the above-mentioned problems, but merely knowing what was wrong did not provide ways to resolve the problems. Nevertheless, there was a new development: consider a strategy to reckon with the societal problem and reach a goal. The use of violent means became a justified strategy. Terrorism began to emerge, and crueler types of terrorist attacks were justified.

The French Revolution in 1789 opened a Pandora's box for a number of revolutionary ideas and actions. It was also in this context that terror was used in a political context for the first time, in a period known as "the Reign of Terror" (1793–1794). Moreover, the Revolution gave birth to armed forces based on conscription and a new and powerful ideology—nationalism. Other ideas that would come to be repeated in other periods and contexts began to be voiced. For example, the Italian-born French revolutionary Filippo Buonarroti (1761–1837) claimed that no means are criminal that are employed for a sacred purpose. Nineteenth-century French anarchist Émile Henry (1872–1894) followed Buonarroti's footsteps and declared that innocent bourgeoisie did not exist. The utopist socialists of the early nineteenth century took the next step: they established the aim for political change, the utopia.

The term "utopia" was first described by Sir Thomas More in 1516, meaning an imagined perfect place or situation like heaven on earth. As the term suggests, neither the aim nor the means to get there were clearly defined. Even Karl Marx (1818–1883) was not able to characterize the essence of his utopic aim, the communist society. Yet, he came out with explicit definitions of the historical force driving it, the enemy and the means for making his aim a reality. The new historical force was the working class, the enemy the capitalist or bourgeoisie class, and the way to reach the new society was the revolution. Thus, for the first time there was a compact package for launching violent actions for political purposes. It was right to kill the capitalists and, in a wider sense, also members of the bourgeoisie class as some sort of collateral damage of the proletariat revolution.

For Karl Marx the enemies were clearly, and in a sense also narrowly, defined, but later this changed. During the second half of the nineteenth century the anarchists continued from the point where Marx had ceased pondering about violence and its targets for political purposes. To put it simply, for Marx the enemy was the capitalist class; the way out of the problem was the revolution and the elimination of the capitalist class. For anarchists everything in the present society was wrong and total anarchy was the only way to achieve a right society. Consequently, everybody—ordinary people included—became a justified target. Yet the main focus of the anarchist was to kill the heads of states, because for them the state was an institution for organized violence used by the ruling class. There it was: because the other party used violence, it was also right for the anarchist to kill people. Laurent Tailharde (1854–1919), a French satirical poet and also an anarchist, claimed that the victims did not matter once the action itself was beautiful (Burleigh 2009).

When we now look at modern terrorism since 1968, we see that there are clear connections between it and the founding fathers of both Marxism and the anarchism of the nineteenth century. The Marxist (or Maoist or Trotskyite) terrorists openly swore by the name of those men, and of course, Lenin. Moreover, they defined their enemies accordingly: they were the capitalists, their supporters and the politicians running the capitalist state. These terrorists' aim was revolution by violent means. They wanted to start a spiral of violence which would, in the end, create a revolutionary situation resulting in a new brave communist society. When they defined their enemies, targets of justified killing, "reasonably," precisely and narrowly, they killed only top politicians and industrial leaders. Thus, the majority of people were safe and the number of victims was low. For example, the German Baader-Meinhof Group killed about thirty people through its terroristic activities.

While the ideological foundations of Islamist jihadist terrorism trace back to certain Islamic teachings and traditions, jihadist terrorism has clearly adapted some of the ideas of the founding fathers of Marxism and, above all, anarchism. The biggest difference between Marxists and anarchists was this: the Marxist terrorists felt justified to kill only certain people, thereby limiting their number of victims. For the anarchists, anybody could be a target. Jihadists have preferred the anarchists' model and consequently, killing anybody has become justified.

In 2000 the Manchester Metropolitan Police found a handwritten document belonging to an al-Qaeda member—"Military Studies in the Jihad against the Tyrants (or Declaration of Jihad against the Country's Tyrants)." The United States Department of Justice translated this from Arabic to English and named it "Al-Qaeda Training Manual," although the document does not mention al-Qaeda and was most probably written before the group's establishment (Thornton 2009). Its only connection to al-Qaeda is that the man in Manchester who had the document was a member of al-Qaeda. The document has clear similarities to ideas presented by Brazilian Marxist Carlos Marighella in his *Minimanual of the Urban Guerilla* (1969). Neither Marighella nor the document called their activities terrorism, but (urban) guerrilla. The main mission of the document is "the overthrow of godless regimes and their replacement with an Islamic regime" (United States Department of Justice translation, p. 13). It also calls for the assassinations of foreign tourists, and "beating and killing the hostages" (United States Department of Justice translation, p. 17).

For Marighella the justification for violence arises from the evils of the society: "Urban guerrilla defends a just cause, which is the people's cause." For the Jihadists the justification comes from God: "We ... with God's help ... call on every Muslim who believes in God and wishes to be rewarded to comply with God's order to kill the Americans and plunder their money wherever and whenever they find it" (Post 2004, p. XIII). For the Jihadists it is justifiable to kill atheists and infidels and accept killing some Muslims as "collateral damage." For example, in the September 11 attacks about thirty Muslims were among those the terrorists killed.

Bin Laden's goal was to establish a global caliphate. Abu Bakr al-

Baghdadi calls himself a caliph (Caliph Ibrahim) and commander of ISIS. We think that there is a major difference here. It is said that Caliph Ibrahim is descended from the tribe of the Prophet, the Quraysh. This, in a sense, "legitimizes" his being a caliph. Unlike Osama bin Laden, the ISIS leader al-Baghdadi and his followers have extended the concept of justified killing from atheists and infidels to "non-Islamic apostate" Muslims (e.g., Shias). Al-Baghdadi represents a Salafist interpretation of Islam based on the teachings of Ibn Taymiyyah (thirteenth century). There is very little the general public in the Western world knows about al-Baghdadi because he keeps a low profile. This reminds us of the Muslim custom of not painting human figures and not making a drawing of Muhammad. There is a possibility that the lack of pictures of al-Baghdadi in social media makes him an even stronger and more holy figure for his diaspora followers. This aligns with the efforts of ISIS in creating a mythology and in offering "glory" for people, especially estranged young, in its recruitment efforts.

At the end of March 2016 President Barack Obama hosted his last nuclear security summit in Washington, DC, attended by a dozen world leaders. The prospect of al-Qaeda and ISIS gaining access to nuclear weapons was on the table. Referring to al-Qaeda and ISIS, Obama said, "There is no doubt that if these mad men ever got their hands on a nuclear bomb or nuclear material, they would certainly use it to kill as many people as possible."

New forms of technology have opened the door for other forms of terrorism, such as cyber terrorism. One such politically motivated attack happened in 2007 when the Estonians moved an old Soviet war memorial, the Bronze Soldier, from the Tallinn city center to a cemetery. As a result, the Estonian state offices and their Internet services were paralyzed by a hostile attack.

Terrorists need not always kill to terrorize, especially when they treat people as economic assets. Victims can become slaves or be sold, and they can also be ransomed. ISIS and Boko Haram engage in slavery (especially using girls as sex slaves) and kidnapping on a wide scale. For example, in April 2014 Boko Haram abducted 276 schoolgirls from Chibok in northeastern Nigeria. After the abduction Boko Haram declared that the girls would be married to the fighters, and those who were not willing to do so would be killed. Also Abubakar Shekau, the leader of Boko Haram, claimed that the girls would be sold into slavery (Hammer 2016). Fifty-seven of these girls were able to escape. The rest were used for the above purposes, and some of them are even brainwashed into becoming Boko Haram fighters (Smith 2015). Inside Cameroon, Boko Haram has also used young girls under sixteen as suicide bombers. Because the bombs were hidden under *burkhas*, Cameroon has banned *burkhas* in the Maroua region. Furthermore, those cases have poisoned the social atmosphere, because young girls are now seen as a threat (Hammer 2016). Most recently, Boko Haram, after prolonged negotiations (and probably the payment of a large ransom), freed eighty-two of these young girls. Many more, however, remain captive.

With ISIS the most brutal case involves the slavery of Iraqi Yazidi girls and women (some figures indicate as many as 5,000 of them) who were abducted in August 2014. Some of them have been able to escape and have told terrible stories of their ordeal. One girl was sold four times and raped by all her "owners" (Dearden 2016). As of April 2016, there are still about 2,000 Yazidi women in ISIS captivity. Human Rights Watch researcher Skye Wheeler hits the nail on the head when asking why we talk only about the destruction of ancient sites such as Palmyra, while the plight of those women is almost totally neglected (Wheeler 2016).

4

FROM MARXISTS TO JIHADISTS

The Bulge Model

Over the last 150 years there have been four waves of politically motivated violence. Toward the end of the nineteenth century and the beginning of the twentieth there were the anarchists who made the turn of the century the most lethal period of all times for heads of state and other political leaders. For example, the most famous political assassination in Finnish history happened in 1904 when Eugen Schauman, a Finnish nationalist and nobleman, shot the Russian Governor-General of Finland, Nikolai Bobrikov. Nationalism reached Africa as an ideology after World War I, and the second wave of politically motivated violence was conducted by anticolonialists after World War II. During the 1960s the Marxists came into the picture, followed by the jihadists after 1979. Marxists and jihadists played major roles in creating third and fourth waves of violence, ideological and religious, both with certain separatist undercurrents.

It is difficult to separate religious terrorism from ideological terrorism. In a sense, all terrorist movements are ideological, even when religion is hijacked for violence. There is a wide spectrum of ideologies: Aum Shinrikyo's "dystopic utopism"; Brigate Rosse's (Red Brigades'), Baader-Meinhof's and FARC's Marxism; Nuclei Armati Rivoluzionari's and

National Socialistic Underground's fascism; and ETA's, IRA's and Tamil Tigers' ethnonationalism (separatism). Religions, contrary to the above-mentioned "earthly" ideologies, are spiritual "heavenly" ideologies, exemplified by the Lord's Resistance Army and Army of God (Christian) and al-Qaeda and ISIS (Muslim). Nonreligious and religious ideological movements tend to draw their fundamental principles from scripture of one form or another, be it *das Kapital* or the Bible or Quran. Religions are often built around a revelation, whereas the political movements prefer to refer to some sort of scientific analysis of society. Yet, earthly aims direct the actions of both types of ideologies. Ideologies are used to motivate their followers to fight and die. In order to illustrate this let us take a look at the Palestinian example, which has been one of the most dominant in the history of modern terrorism.

The Palestinians' aim is to establish an independent Palestinian state. Their actions on a general level can be classified as separatist. Based on the earlier Zionist models (such as Irgun and Stern Gang), the Palestinians made a strategic choice to resort to terrorism in the mid-1960s. The first tactical choice for ideology of the Popular Front for the Liberation of Palestine (PFLP) was secularism (al-Fatah), or even Marxism. When secularism/Marxism as a motivating ideology ran into the sand over the next two decades, a new one came to the fore in the late 1980s—namely, Islamism or jihadism. With it, the nature of their terrorism evolved.

Based on the statistics of the Peace Research Institute of Oslo (PRIO) and Uppsala Conflict Data Program (UCDP) there has recently been a worldwide declining trend in the number of armed conflicts and their victims. Yet, this view has been challenged by some scholars, such as Jeffrey Lewis (2015), an American expert in nuclear nonproliferation and geopolitics. The victims of internal violence in Muslim-majority countries (such as in Afghanistan, Iraq, Somalia, Syria and Turkey) include civilians, and often the number of deaths of innocent persons is greater than of military ones. This pushed the overall balance between the numbers of military and civilian victims toward the civilian end. Some sources even suggest that 90 percent of victims in such countries are civilians; others say 60 percent (Roberts 2010).

There is good reason to presume that terrorism during the last five decades is connected to the huge cultural, political, social and technological changes that took place after the Second World War. This transition marked the coming of the information society, or globalization. Its impact on large-group identity has played a significant role in the mushrooming of terrorism.

In 1962 Marshall McLuhan coined the term "global village," meaning the shrinking of the globe into a metaphorical village. This shrinking was due to two developments, one in mobility and the other in communication. It was now much cheaper and easier to travel to and also to receive information from far ends of the globe. Inevitably, events the world over through satellite channels, Internet and social media became almost as local as those in one's home village, and people began learning about faraway events as they were happening. Theoretically speaking, globalization can be called a meta-system: a system that describes, analyses, and creates models for and changes in subsystems—economic, political, social and cultural. The connecting link, or the conveyor belt, between globalization and these subsystems was technology. Satellite channels started to pop up around 1990. At the same time the number of mobile phone and Internet users began to increase dramatically. Finally social media became widely used in the 2000s. In a 2015 study of a group of Arab youths, for example, about 77 percent had smart phones and 82 percent used the Internet daily (7th Annual ASDA'A Burson-Marsteller Arab Youth Survey, 2015).

Peter Neumann, professor of security studies in the Department of War Studies at King's College, in his book *Old and New Terrorism: Late Modernity, Globalization and the Transformation of Political Violence* (2009), relates how two British scholars, David Held and Anthony McGrew, saw four processes in globalization: (1) extensity: being active beyond national borders; (2) velocity: speeding up global interactions; (3) intensity: intensifying activities; and (4) impact: reaching distant decision making and events. These four processes have caused feelings of uncertainty and inability to be a master of one's own life, and what's more, they have challenged large-group identities and played a role in increasing terrorism.

These processes all have bearing on the question, "Who are we now?" The answer for some has been to pursue a kind of escapism—a return to values believed to be "old and solid," fundamentalist interpretations of religions included. This type of response helped prepare the ground for religious radicalism and caused a polarization in societies between those who wish to reclaim a glorified past, whether real or imagined, and those who do not want to follow this path. This polarization is clearly visible in Turkey today.

Still, religious fundamentalism and jihadism do not totally contradict modernity. The view that jihadism and modernity are in binary opposition (jihad versus McWorld) should be replaced with the view that "jihad is not only McWorld's adversary, it is its child" (Neumann 2009, pp. 87–88). Indeed, modernity has recently influenced the rise of terrorism in several ways: communication technology spreads ideas and ideologies; communication helps build and keep terrorist organizations active; and finally, communication has shaken traditional and often authoritarian societies and made them vulnerable to political violence. Martha Crenshaw, a professor of political science at Stanford University, connects modern terrorism with the large urbanization process of the last two hundred years. Big cities formed a new type of space where people were able to come together and unite for a common cause behind roadblocks or form an urban guerrilla or terrorist group. Crenshaw also points out that there is a high number of first-class targets—such as metros—for terrorists in urban centers, and unfortunately, a high number of people in public places can be murdered *en masse* (2011).

Jouni Suistola has developed what he calls the *Bulge Model* to enlighten us about the relations between ideological change and the emergence of terrorism in a society. In developing this model one of his starting points is Peter Neumann's argument that "terrorist political ideas always tend to reflect a given society's radical ideological currents" and that the "majority of terrorist groups are often rooted in conventional political activism and discourses" (2009 p. 20). The development of terrorism can be crystallized into two consequential steps: first ideological radicalization occurs and then it is followed by a strategic choice. The simple logic of the Bulge Model is as follows: the more people in general move to support a radical ideology, creating a "bulge," the more individuals adopt terrorism as their strategic choice. Now we present two applications of the model, in Marxist and jihadist forms of terrorism.

FIGURE 1. BULGE OF POLITICAL RADICALIZATION IN THE LATE 1960S

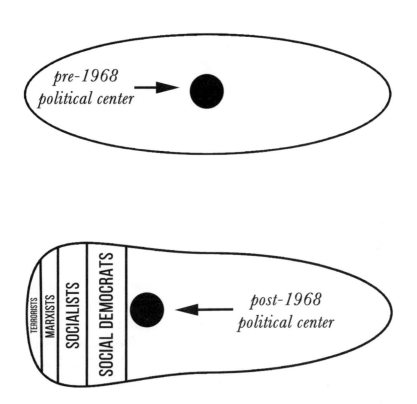

The Marxist terrorism movement began in 1968 on university campuses in the Western world. The first step was students becoming radicalized, moving to the left and forming there a bulge (see figure 1). With the bulge the whole political spectrum became heavily left-leaning in nature, and a high number of leftist young people then faced the question of how to change, or fight and destroy, the bourgeoisie class society. That was the moment of strategic choice and some—in fact, not very many—of them chose terrorism.

The emergence of Islamist jihadists follows the same pattern, although the time frame for its happening has taken much longer: the radical leftist movement turned to terrorism inside of a few months, whereas in the case of jihadism it took decades. The origins of jihadism go back to the emergence of the fundamentalist interpretation of Islam. There seems to be a consensus that Ibn Taymiyyah (born in 1263 in Eastern Anatolia) is the founding father of Islamic fundamentalism. Most notably, his idea of *takfir*, which allows one Muslim to declare another Muslim an infidel (*kafir*), has been the core of intrafaith violence inside Islam. Ibn Taymiyyah's teachings became the basis for the ideas of Muhammad Ibn Abd al-Wahhab, an eighteenth-century scholar on the Arabian Peninsula. Ibn Abd al-Wahhab's views later evolved as the official Saudi interpretation of Islam called Wahhabism. From an organizational perspective, the next important step was taken in 1928 when an Egyptian Islamic scholar, Hassan al-Banna, established the Muslim Brotherhood, which at its inception acted within the frames of a "normal," although strict, interpretation of Islam. The transformation of the Muslim Brotherhood toward political Islam was made in the 1950s and 1960s by an Egyptian teacher, Sayyid Qutb. A parallel step toward political Islam was taken in India (and after 1947 in Pakistan) by Imam Abu A'la Maududi, who founded Jamaat-e-Islami in 1941.

The Saudi-supported Salafist or Wahhabi interpretation of Islam expanded the reach of fundamentalist Sunni Islam, while the Iranian revolution of 1979 strengthened fundamentalist Shia Islam. (There are no doctrinal differences between Salafism and Wahhabism. Salafism is based on the teachings of Ibn Taymiyyah, while Wahhabism is based on the teachings of al-Wahhab, the founder of the "state religion" of Saudi Arabia. When Saudis support the expansion of their version of Islam abroad we usually call it Salafism.) By the late 1970s the fundamentalist-Islamist bulge was present, even as competition between Sunnis and Shia grew. The center of Islam or mainstream Islam had moved to the political left, or political right, if you like, as radical Islam cannot be easily placed on a Western-oriented political spectrum (see figure 2). The clash between Shi'ites and Sunnis can be compared to the clash between different orientations of the extreme left, such as Marxism, Maoism or Trotskyism. With growing numbers of radicalized Muslims, it was time for a strategic choice, which for many often competing radical Islamist groups came in the form of terrorism.

This growing fundamentalist-Islamist bulge spread to Central Asia. The Soviet Union's occupation of Afghanistan in 1979 triggered a strengthening

FIGURE 2. BULGE OF MUSLIM RADICALIZATION AFTER 1979

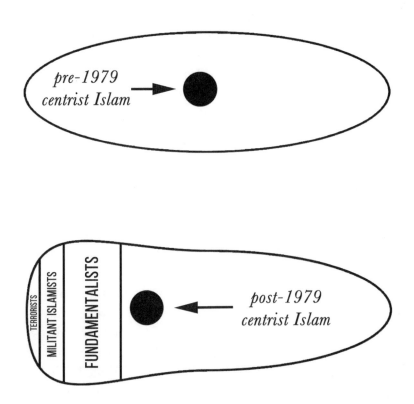

insurgence that attracted radicalized Muslims from Arab countries to join the fight against the Soviet infidels. This movement developed side by side with the United States' efforts to construct a barrier against the Soviet Union along the Soviet's southern flank. This strategy, known as the green belt strategy, in reference to the color most associated with Islam, aimed to increase investment in Islam in the swath of Muslim-majority countries between Greece and China. Those who imagined and implemented this strategy hoped both to stop the spread of Soviet influence and to inflame Muslims within the Soviet Union to undermine the Soviet Empire from the inside. Religious education served a key role in this strategy.

Islamic schools (madrassas) for children and youth have existed since the beginning of Islam. The green belt strategy, however, greatly increased their number, especially in Pakistan. What was different about these new Pakistani madrassas, funded by the United States as well as Great Britain, was their inclusion of training in the service of future violence. With financial support coming from the Saudis, these madrassas were influenced by the Wahhabist/Salafist and Deobandi versions of extreme religious "ideology" (Rashid 2000). (Deobandi comes from the name of a city in India, Deoband, about 150 kilometers from Delhi. The Deobandi movement began in 1867 after a failed revolt against British rule.)

The children in the madrassas learned to recite the Quran in Arabic, but since they did not know Arabic, they had to accept the "interpretation" given to them by their teachers. For example, when they read in Urdu, they were told that the Urdu letter *jeem* stood for jihad; *kaaf* for Kalashnikov and *khy* for khoon (blood) (Ali 2001). The "graduates" of these madrassas would later help to create a foundation on which the Taliban and al-Qaeda could stand, along with the many so-called Afghan Arabs who had fought in Afghanistan.

In the 1980s the number of foreign fighters in Afghanistan reached about 25,000. The Saudis and Americans financed the *mujahideen*, a term used for Muslim fighters engaged in jihad. The Pakistani Inter-Services Intelligence trained about 80,000 fighters, and the Americans armed them. Together with their radical interpretation of Islam, those battle-hardened fighters comprised a lethal cocktail. When the war against the Soviets was over in 1989 they made a strategic choice for the coming battles elsewhere, and the choice was terrorism. The *Al-Qaeda Training Manual* stresses that the principle enemies of the *mujahideen* were corrupt Middle Eastern governments and authoritarian rulers. Only later did they begin to pay attention to fighting the West.

5

THE SOCIO-POLITICAL CONFLICT AND TERRORISM

A stable society rarely gives birth to terrorism, but cannot escape from it completely. For example, after 1968, Marxist terrorism hit Germany and Italy, two otherwise stable societies. Terrorism usually occurs when a conflict initiated within a large group itself, or by an external influence, derails societal stability. By "conflict," we are referring not only to ethnic or political conflicts but also to economic and social conflicts. Indeed, while a lack of human or political rights is often the principal catalyst of terrorism, it is not the only catalyst. For instance, poverty—more particularly, uneven distribution of wealth, youth unemployment, inhuman living conditions, marginalization and corruption—can be a driver of terrorism.

When a conflict derails a society's stability, people may reconcile themselves to the situation, resist it or even try to escape to other locations. To resist societal instability, people have three basic choices: to push for change within the established political and economic system; to take to the streets and public squares—as happened during the collapse of the Soviet Empire in 1989–1991 and the Arab Spring in December 2010 in Tunisia; or to resort to armed resistance, such as through terrorism. Although each choice is markedly different, all are in one form or another responses to a set of destabilizing socio-political problems or grievances (see figure 3).

FIGURE 3. SOCIO-POLITICAL CONFLICT AND ITS CONSEQUENCES

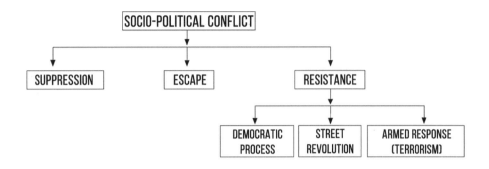

Economic conflict, ranging from poverty to uneven distribution of wealth to lack of opportunities, has been a favorite explanation for terrorism by many politicians, including George W. Bush in 2002 and Tony Blair in 2004. In 2014, Tunisian president Beji Caid Essebsi declared, "We must confront the fact that poverty is producing terrorism." Yet, studies made over the past decade claim that economic factors do not play a significant role in the development of terrorism (Krueger 2007; Lutz and Lutz 2008; Berman 2009). Allan B. Krueger (2007) argues that the uneducated and poor are particularly unlikely to participate in terroristic activities and that terrorists typically come from educated middle- or even high-income classes. To support his view, Krueger refers to the work of a United Nation relief worker, Nasra Hassan. In the early 2000s Hassan interviewed 250 Palestinian militants and their associates and concluded that none of them "were uneducated, desperately poor … Many were middle class …, and held paying jobs" (Krueger 2007, pp. 32–33). Krueger also describes Claude Berrebi's work with Palestinian suicide bombers. Only a few of them were from families below the poverty line. Less than 15 percent of the general Palestinian population had more than a high school degree; among the bombers the rate was 60 percent.

Even though these findings indicate that most Palestinian suicide bombers of the early 2000s were not from families below the poverty line, the issue of poverty and education in a society needs a closer look. It may not be poverty or a low-level of education that matters. If almost everyone in a certain society is poor and poorly educated, this might not seed terrorism. But, if a minority of a society's members is rich and well-educated and the rest are poor and illiterate and there is a vast class difference, as Marxists would say, this situation certainly would be a problem; it would provide fertile ground for terrorism. Martha Crenshaw (2011) pays attention to the role a group of individuals who perceive they are being treated in a discriminatory and unjust way play in initiating societal trouble.

Even when social stability is maintained by an oppressive government and by force, the probability of terrorism is relatively low. The Soviet Union, Somalia, Afghanistan, Iraq and Syria were good examples of this type of stability. If something derails the stability, terrorism emerges. In the case of the Soviet Union it was the collapse of the state in 1991. In Somalia it was the ousting of a military dictator, President Siad Barre, which turned Somalia into a failed state. In Afghanistan and Iraq it was the U.S.-led interventions. In Syria everything started in March 2011 in the wake of the Arab Spring when the people in the Deraa region began demonstrations and the government responded with a military attack on civilians, killing many. Authoritarian regimes and dictatorships often rely on strong-arm tactics to suppress terrorism that more democratic governments are not able to use on their own citizens (at least not openly), especially with regard to widespread warrantless surveillance and searches, torture, unlawful detention, and even extrajudicial killings.

The social context from which terrorist groups have arisen varies considerably. For example, al-Qaeda began as a small organization led by educated and even privileged elites. Osama bin Laden came from a very wealthy family and studied at university. Ayman al-Zawahiri, the current leader of al-Qaeda, is a medical doctor. Some groups, meanwhile, for example, the Revolutionary Armed Forces of Colombia (FARC), established in 1964 as the military wing of the Colombian Communist Party, spring from a rural population with grievances against a central government. The Irish Republican members were very often from the working class, as were the members of the Italian Brigate Rosse. Some terrorist organizations, such as Taliban, Haqqani Network and al-Shabaab, have strong tribal connections and, thus, by extension, likely share the same social strata as the tribes to which the members belong.

In light of the November 13, 2015 Paris and March 22, 2016 Brussels terrorist attacks we see an additional social context of terrorism. Muslims in France and Belgium are mostly of Northern African origin. In Belgium they are mainly descendants of Moroccan immigrants of the 1960s. Almost all of the March 2004 attackers in Madrid had links to the Moroccan Rif region, as did the terrorists in Brussels. These terrorists had ties to the Brussels district of Molenbeek, known as "the Rotten Heart of Europe" (Jacinto 2016a, p.1). The unemployment rate in Belgium is about 8 percent, but for the citizens of Moroccan origin it is estimated to be around 40 percent. The population In Molenbeek is especially alienated, marginalized and poor and thus susceptible to the messages and promises of criminal or radical organizations. International news reporter Leela Jacinto (2016b) informs us, those from the Rif region of Morocco have a long history of resistance against authorities, from colonial masters to many others. In the background of their terrorist networks are networks constructed for other, basically criminal, purposes. It is a well-known fact that during the last couple of years Belgium has become an "arms depot" for terrorist cells. In sum, the terrorists connected with the Rif region had already crossed many lines on the way to terrorism, and there were only two more lines to cross: religious radicalization and violence. This is not to say that all people of Molenbeek are terrorists; only a handful of them are. However, networks supportive of terrorism exist there, as we saw in the case of Salah Abdeslam, one of the November 2015 operatives in Paris (and the only survivor), who was able to hide in Molenbeek with the support of his friends until March 2016.

As the above cases demonstrate, various factors or combinations of factors prepare a fertile ground for terrorism to emerge, whether related to a lack of political rights, civil liberties, economic opportunities, or freedom of expression among others. But once seeded, how does it spread or spill over into other countries or regions?

In broad terms, terrorism spills over into other territories in one of two ways: strongly or weakly. When a terrorist organization or one of its branches strategically executes a terrorist act outside of its original operational territory, this is classified as representing a "strong" spillover.

For example, an article in *The Economist* (July 4, 2015) titled "Islamic State: Spreading Its Tentacles" describes the strong spillover of ISIS. It is spreading strategic or core operations through Iraq and Syria and, at the same time, it appears also to encompass Saudi Arabia, Algeria, Egypt, Libya, Yemen, North-East Nigeria, Pakistan, Afghanistan and lately also the Caucasus. In an innovative organizational step forward, it claims statehood in Syria and Iraq (IS, Islamic State) and, as the next step, moves toward a federated state or a provincial system based on new "provinces" of the caliphate. The caliphate applies strict rules to qualify as a province: it must have a governor and a ruling council, it must follow the ISIS' version of Islamic rule, and it must have a plan for territorial conquest.

Here are three more examples of strong spillover: in 2004, a Chechen terrorist group raided a school in the North Ossetian city of Beslan, which ultimately led to the death of 385 people, most of them schoolchildren; in 2013, the Somalian terrorist organization al-Shabaab attacked a shopping mall in Kenya and killed sixty-seven people; and in 2015 during an attack on Garissa University College, Kenya the same organization killed 147 people.

A "weak" spillover means that the connection between the original terrorist organization and the overseas operations and organizations is loose. Seen from the perspective of the core organization, we can talk about active and passive spillover. In an active weak spillover the original organization offers a model for how to organize and how to fight and attack. It also encourages copycats and lone wolves to act without any solid connection to the original organization. In a passive spillover the person or people committing the terrorist act draw inspiration from another terrorist organization but take their own tactical initiative.

Here are three examples of weak spillover: in December 2001, Richard Reid tried to bring down an airliner with the explosives in his shoes, but he had only a loose connection to al-Qaeda and was inspired by hate-speech in a British mosque; in April 2013, the Tsarnaev brothers bombed the Boston Marathon but had no known organizational connections to terrorist groups; and in June 2016, Omar Mateen attacked Pulse, a popular gay nightclub in Orlando, killing forty-nine and wounding fifty-three people. Although the twenty-nine-year-old Mateen professed allegiance to ISIS, and ISIS was quick to claim responsibility for the attack, CIA director John Brennan said after the attack that no actual links between the attacker and the terrorist organization had yet been uncovered.

Indeed, ISIS has called on sympathizers to carry out attacks in their home countries. A terrorist organization can also run a propaganda or hate-speech campaign to rally support and to recruit new members. In the 1970s Ayatollah Ruhollah Khomeini (1902–1989) depended on long-distance telephone calls and taped recordings to spread his religious fundamentalist revolution. Today, terrorist groups can spread their political propaganda to every corner of the globe through the Internet and social media.

6

POLITICAL PROPAGANDA

Political propaganda, in its widest definition, encompasses any communication or manipulation from a source of authority that is directed toward followers, opponents, and/or "neutrals" or "bystanders." Its aim is to further the wishes and ideas of the propagandist, which may be a government or an organization, a president or an insurgent, a general or a terrorist. Political propaganda exists in all politically organized societies, whether open or closed.

The historical precursors to political propaganda may be the tribal battle sounds of earlier times "meant to encourage one's own group, frighten the foe, and impress those who did not participate in fight" (Kris 1943, p. 282). The war cry known as *alala*, accompanied by nonverbal symbols such as banners and uniforms, is said to have been a significant battlefield tool for the ancient Greeks. During the Persian Wars in the fifth century BCE, the Athenian leader Themistocles carved on beach cliffs descriptions of the horrors waiting for Persian soldiers inside Greek territory. The ancient Roman armies used shouts and accompanying trumpet blasts called *clamor* and later adapted the Teutonic battle cry *barditus*: "Tacitus describes it as an explosion of raucous sounds, made more prolonged and more resounding by pressing the shield against the mouth" (Chakotin 1939, p.

34). Beginning as a murmur, it would steadily grow louder, rousing intense excitement within the fighting men.

As time went on, other means of influencing feelings and behavior and generating support for political and military decisions and actions in times of conflict superseded the battle sounds, and the use of such methods in peacetime as well as in war became more common. The appearance of propaganda in its broadest sense became more closely connected with religious issues. The battle cry of the Ottomans employed their God's name as if their side was sanctioned by God and that He would take care of any Ottoman soldier killed in battle. Ottoman Janissaries shouted "Allah! Allah!" as their colorful marching band, the *Mehter*, provided resounding martial music. As a description of the Ottoman Army published in Vienna in 1683 put it, "Mehter music empowers even camels to march better" (Türkisch Stats- und Kriegsbericht No 3. Das beladene Kamel. Wien 1683).

About twenty years ago Vamık Volkan was attending an international meeting in Istanbul with hundreds of participants from different countries. One evening, the Turkish hosts gave a big dinner party in the gardens of the Turkish Military Museum, and everyone was having a very good time. Then the Turks entertained the guests by having a group of men dressed in Janissary uniforms play *Mehte*r music. When they appeared with their drums and horns and began calling their God's name, "Allah! Allah!" some guests from the Balkans literally had an anxiety attack and left the party. The religious battle cry of the past and the music that accompanied it was frightening to the descendants of a "victimized" large group even centuries later.

Historically, Christians have not been immune from using religion as a propaganda tool for their own ends either. Garth Jowett and Victoria O'Donnell (1992) wrote about how the concept of "propagating" (propaganda derives from the Latin "to propagate") first lost its neutrality in 1622. That year the Vatican established the *Sacra Congregatio de Propaganda Fide* (the "Sacred Congregation for Propagating the Faith") of the Roman Catholic Church. As its purpose was to spread Catholicism throughout the New World at the expense of the "reformed" faiths, the term "propaganda" then became a pejorative term in Protestant Western Europe.

In the early 1800s a new "science" called hypnotism became all the rage in Europe when Viennese physician Franz Anton Mesmer appeared on the scene, fascinating audiences from nobles to scientists with his demonstrations. The influence of hypnotism endured even after a commission of the French Academy of Sciences declared Mesmer a charlatan. Decades later another Frenchman, social psychologist Gustave Le Bon, published a book *The Crowd: A Study of Popular Mind* (1895), which echoed the dynamics of hypnotism. Le Bon explored how individuals lose their distinctiveness when operating in a crowd, acquiescing to group consensus. This can easily be observed, even in a functional group like a marching band that operates as a unit with a common purpose. Individuality is displaced by common identity and the actions of the individual are evaluated only as they relate to the group's mission. With the exception of some small groups in which participants interact more intimately, Le Bon found that crowds crave illusions. If a leader can supply these illusions, he or she can use them to manipulate and control a crowd—much as a hypnotist would (Volkan 2013). One can see Le Bon's influence on Sigmund Freud's psychoanalytic ideas about large groups (Freud 1921), but what is less known to psychoanalysts is Le Bon's influence on the development of modern *malignant* propaganda. After a trip to India, Le Bon came up with the notion that the white race was in danger, and wrote the book *The Psychology of Politics and Social Defense* (1910). His work helped lay the groundwork for fascist theories.

Harrold Lasswell (1938), a pioneer in the study of psychosocial warfare, views World War I (1914–1918) as the beginning of the "discovery of propaganda by both the man in the street and the man in the study." At the outbreak of the war there was no public scrutiny of secret diplomacy or interest in oppressed large groups of people. Soldiers were professionals who had little animosity toward the enemy they were killing and knew little about why they were fighting. A good portrayal of this was the 1981 Australian film *Gallipoli* directed by Peter Weir (starring Mel Gibson). As this war progressed, however—with rising casualties, domestic privations and monetary cost—it began to more directly affect people. There was a need to encourage both public support and the soldiers' will to continue fighting, and this became evident in public rhetoric. Vague and lofty language inflated reports of victories and encouraged the public with phrases such as "self-determination" and "the war to end all wars" (Brown 1963, p. 91). Lasswell (1938) thus argued that propaganda was "discovered" at this time and was more startling, he said, to the man in the street than to the man in the study.

New technology had an impact as well on the use of propaganda in World War I. Besides relying on the dissemination and distribution of printed material, the parties to this war were able to utilize telegraphs and telephones and wireless radio. Fledgling motion picture technology also played a role in war propaganda for the first time. Although Germany was slow to adopt it for propaganda, by the 1930s, Germany had developed a highly effective propaganda machine using the well-known work of filmmaker Leni Riefenstahl and others.

Adolf Hitler understood the power of political propaganda, devoting two chapters to its proper design and execution in *Mein Kampf.* It should be aimed, he said, "only to a limited degree at the so-called intellect ... The art of propaganda lies in understanding the emotional ideas of great masses and finding through a psychologically correct form, the way to attention and hence to the heart of the broad masses" (Hitler 1925–1926, p. 180). Hitler's image and many of his signature gestures were created for effect, and much credit for their success went to his confederate, Joseph Goebbels, a master of propaganda (Reimann 1976; Volkan, Ast, and Greer 2002).

Le Bon's ideas from years earlier were not lost on the WWII generation. Psychoanalyst Ernst Kris (1943) wrote: "The student of history of ideas will note in Le Bon the parallel with Nietzsche and reaction to Marx, but he will also be able to quote chapter and verse in order to prove how closely statements by Le Bon reappear in the concepts of propaganda developed by Hitler and Goebbels" (p. 388). When Benito Mussolini came to power in Italy, he spoke in admiration of Le Bon's ideas and said they had influenced him. Le Bon, then almost ninety years old, praised Mussolini in turn, saying that he admired Italy's "new order."

In response to the political and economic humiliation experienced by Germany following World War I, Nazi propaganda created a shared psychic reality aiming to boost the German people's "Aryan" identity while simultaneously dehumanizing the identities of millions of Jews, Roma and others. By building the Fuhrer's omnipotence and fulfilling the German people's need to believe that they were following a great leader, Nazi propaganda lifted their self-esteem and made them feel they were members of a race of super beings. Elsewhere, Volkan (Volkan, Ast, and Greer 2002; Volkan 2013) analyzed the psychology of Nazi propaganda and how it accomplished its mission, including through the creation of disturbances in the family system by severing children and youth from their natural object of love and attachment and then filling this vacuum with collective grandiosity and National Socialist "morality." Volkan also discussed how the image of Hitler was handled by Joseph Goebbels to make it seem that he was a good man who had no hand in any violent atrocities. There were also times when a clearly satisfied Hitler publicly proclaimed his "aggressive triumphs" of a genocidal nature that were carried out in order to protect his super beings from contamination by those deemed subhuman, as if they were dangerous germs. All the historic humiliations and hurts experienced earlier by the German people could be effectively denied in the wake of this Nazi idealism. This ideology was used in place of religion as an emotional tool. However, upon closer scrutiny, since Hitler was presented as a god, can we really differentiate ideological and religious tools for political propaganda as presented by the Nazis?

The Allies' propaganda during World War II, while it emphasized military prowess to distract attention from its defeats, also allowed criticism. After the war there was discussion internationally about specifying legal exceptions to freedom of speech, such as hate speech that incites racism. Because the U.S. Constitution's First Amendment prohibits regulation of any speech unless it is proven to lead to a clear and present danger, the United States did not join in this effort, but in Germany today any hate speech that harms human dignity is banned by law. Israeli law defines incitement as being connected with rebellious acts, which causes legal confusion. Even in democratic nations, it seems, propaganda and free-speech issues still inspire debate.

World over, one can find societies subjected, to one degree or another, to what might be called "malignant" propaganda, sometimes called "brainwashing" or "thought reform" by those in power. As described by psychiatrist Robert Jay Lifton and others, this occurred in China in the lead-up to its revolution, when its world was divided into "good"/"pure" and "bad"/"impure" categories. This might serve as a clinical description of the internal worlds of patients diagnosed with "borderline personality organization". What is pathological for the individual had become the prescribed reform among in China (Lifton 1961; Buckman 1977).

Earlier we mentioned that Iran's Ayatollah Khomeini depended on long-distance telephone calls and tape recorders to spread his religious fundamentalist revolution. In December 1991 ABC's *Nightline* reported on the first recorded use of the fax machine for propaganda purposes in Riyadh. Leaflets describing how to prepare for a chemical warfare assault, presumably sent by Saddam Hussein's propagandists, came through thousands of Saudi Arabian fax machines. Poland's Lech Walesa once commented that the underground Solidarity movement could not have succeeded without video technology. The evermore rapid proliferation of communication technologies during the last several decades and the use of the Internet have predictably diversified the means and methods of political manipulation and influence. Now, in our daily lives we are constantly exposed to political propaganda. For example, in 2015, ISIS members sent about 100,000 tweets a day from 45,000 to 50,000 Twitter accounts. As Rob Wainwright, the director of Europol, claims, the target group of the tweets is young people in the West, and the aim is to recruit young men and women to the rank and file of ISIS (Dodd 2015). The Twitter campaign is actively supported by a huge amount of propaganda on the Internet: in one day the Islamic State circulates on average three new videos and four photographic reports (Rafiq 2015).

When a large group wonders, "Who are we now?" the personality of the political leader or the new leader after a revolution becomes an important factor in the scenario, one that has considerable influence on societal and political processes. The leader may tame or inflame other large-group sentiments; he or she may lead the large group toward peaceful coexistence with Others, or fuel a warlike atmosphere, even playing an actual role in starting a war. Leaders can be reparative or destructive (Post 2015; Volkan 2004, 2009; Volkan and Fowler 2009). A reparative leader tries to increase the followers' narcissistic investment in large-group identity without malignantly devaluating or hurting Others, whether they are within the same legal boundary of the large group to which the leader belongs or outside of this boundary. A destructive leader aims to enhance or modify the large group's identity by destroying, one way or another, including through terrorism, an opposing or devalued group.

Political propaganda effective at creating an atmosphere for malignant action usually does so through a stereotyped pattern (Volkan 2013):

1. Enhancing a shared sense of victimization or an unfair situation within the targeted large group, whether real or imagined;

2. Reactivating a chosen trauma or a past shared trauma;

3. Creating a time collapse that mixes up the image of a past enemy with the present devalued opposing group, whether inside or outside the country;

4. Devaluing the opposing group and dehumanizing it;

5. Presenting the large-group leadership as an omnipotent "savior";

6. Elevating large-group identity to be more important than individual identity, such as through interference with home life and the family system, education in schools and other means;

7. Increasing a sense of "we-ness" (large-group narcissism) that is contaminated with an entitlement ideology usually linked with the reactivated chosen trauma;

8. Expressing preoccupation with the large group's psychological borders through an obsession with physical borders;

9. Turning an entitlement ideology into revengeful actions and thus allowing mass killings to be committed.

For the most part, psychoanalysts have not written a great deal about political propaganda, with a few exceptions: Roger E. Money-Kyrle (1941), Edward Glover (1947) and Vamık Volkan (2013). Ernst Kris (1943, 1944) also wrote about "opinion leaders" who may or may not be official political spokespersons—ministers, doctors or teachers, for example. And he also identified what he called "wicked agitators" who polarize and target according to their own opinions and to enhance their own status.

Although we still recognize these categories, Kris could not have imagined how information technology would streamline political propaganda these many decades later.

7

TERRORIST PROPAGANDA

Selling ISIS

Both terrorists and governments rely on propaganda, with the media often serving as gatekeeper and mediator of information put forward by the parties involved. Terrorists use propaganda with the following goals in mind: to promote their worldview as a religious or political ideology and set of values; to gain publicity and a favorable attitude for their case; to create an image of legitimacy for their organization and justification for their actions; to attract new members and supporters; to counter the propaganda of their enemy; and to terrorize and destabilize the enemy.

Governments use propaganda with their own set of competing goals: to promote the state's worldview and set of values; to promote the international status of the state and to gather support for it; to stress the criminality of terrorist actions; to maintain the monopoly of legitimacy and justification for violent action by the state against terrorism, including possible limitations of political and human rights; and to counter the propaganda of terrorists and to deny it any public platform.

The media, meanwhile, mediate both objective and subjective information on terrorism in an effort "to tell the truth"; to increase the circulation of a newspaper, the audience of a television or radio program, or the page views of a website; to promote the political agenda or ideology of owners of media; and to protect freedom of expression.

When we take a look at the development of modern terrorism since the 1960s, we note that the evolution of terrorist propaganda went hand in hand with the evolution of terrorist tactics. At the same time the evolution of terrorist propaganda reflected the relationship between the terrorist organization and the media and societies involved. Terrorists wanted their extreme movements to be heard and their profile to be raised. Thus, their ideologies became more extreme and their actions—"propaganda of deed"—became more spectacular, brutal and inhumane. Sometimes such actions even led to "cultural genocide," such as the one conducted by ISIS in Palmyra, Syria.

The Popular Front for the Liberation of Palestine (PFLP) was the pioneer of both international terrorism propaganda and modern "propaganda of deed." The PFLP hijacked sixteen planes between 1968 and 1976. These events made front-page news and brought international attention to the Middle Eastern conflict.

In the propaganda war, terrorists' targets, such as the World Trade Center towers in New York and the Pentagon on September 11, 2001, are often selected according to their symbolic value. By doing so the terrorists aim to say, "We are able to hit the heart of our enemy." This, in turn, amplifies the group's exposure and message. For example, the actions of Black September, a Palestinian Liberation Organization (PLO)–related terrorist organization, during the 1972 Summer Olympics in Munich became a milestone for global media coverage of terrorism.

Not only do terrorist organizations consider propaganda value in selecting their targets, but so do those terrorists with loose connections to such organizations, the lone wolves. For example, *Jyllands-Posten* newspaper in Aarhus, Denmark, in 2005 and *Charlie Hebdo* magazine in Paris, France, in 2015 became targets because they had published anti-Islamic satire. A Kosher grocery store where four persons were killed was targeted during the November 2015 Paris attacks in part because it symbolically represented Zionism. On the same day in Paris a coffee shop, a rock concert and a football stadium also became targets because they represented what the terrorists considered the Western degenerate lifestyle. The ISIS-connected terrorist attack in Istanbul on January 6, 2016 targeted tourists at one of the most visited districts in Turkey, Sultanahmet, killing thirteen. On March 19, 2016 another ISIS-related terrorist attack in Istanbul killed five people, this time in front of the district governor's office.

As integral parts of modern city life, transportation systems are also regularly targeted. A double-decker coach and the London Underground became targets in July 2005. They not only offer crowds of people packed in small spaces but also serve as symbols of London. The underground metros in Delhi, Moscow, Tokyo and Brussels have also been targets, as have airports, including Zaventem Airport in Brussels on March 22, 2016 and Istanbul Atatürk Airport on June 29, 2016.

The main targets for both leftist terrorists and jihadists have been Western society and states. Marxists and Maoists targeted class society, Western democracy and imperialism. Jihadists also see such structures as unjust but frame their narrative through their particular interpretation of Islam. Separatist terrorist groups such as ISIS have a wider framework for propaganda: they also wish to influence members of the ethnic group to which they belong. The goal of the Arab Spring was to establish more democratic political systems and better economic opportunities within Arab countries. The goal of ISIS is to hold on to and grow its self-declared Islamic Caliphate. The goals of the Arab Spring and Western society are thus presented as the same in the propaganda of groups like ISIS. This propaganda also frames Western military operations in the Middle East and Central Asia as attacks on Islam itself.

States by their nature try to maintain a monopoly on the use of violence. There has thus been a tendency to define as terrorism only the violent actions of nonstate actors. It is "understood" that states cannot be terrorists. Governments benefit from their monopoly on violence by referring to their counterterrorist activities as "wars." In September 2001, U.S. President George W. Bush declared a "war on terror," and in November 2015, French President François Hollande stated that France "is at war." Hollande's use of this term helped sell his counterterrorism strategies as being part of a legitimate, organized and structured process. Jihadists also use similar language. In 1998, for example, Osama bin Laden declared a "jihad against Jews and Crusaders." By claiming to be a state, ISIS attempts to create a perception of legitimacy for its violent acts. Earlier, the Irish Republican Army included the term *army* in its title, indicating that it was a party in a civil war, not just a violent gang.

Social environments also affect the nature of terrorist propaganda. Consider the German and Italian versions of ultra-leftist terrorism, RAF Rote Armee Fraktion (RAF) (or Baader-Meinhof-Group) and Brigate Rosse (BR). RAF was clearly a violent extension of the university-based revolution of 1968, and the members were mainly Marxist intellectuals. As a result, their early texts and propaganda were mostly directed to other intellectuals and were primarily theoretical in nature. BR was launched in the industrial centers of Italy, inside big factories, and its members were mainly workers. Thus, it was more like an extension of the ultra-leftist labor movement—at least until 1973 when its attacks on the Italian state began. Consequently, BR's propaganda was more concrete and dealt often with the daily problems of factory workers. Their practical propaganda technique was issuing leaflets produced with a copy machine and distributing them at factory gates. In Torino the standard print run for each leaflet was 10,000 copies. BR also fully employed "propaganda of deed." For example, in 1972, BR militants burned nine cars owned by the most hated directors and guards of the Fiat car factory. This action brought new support and many new members to BR. When the Italian state became the target of BR in the fall of 1973, the propaganda changed accordingly: the contents became more politicized and the target group was the whole Italian nation—if not the whole world. The first major operation was the kidnapping of Genoese judge Mario Sossi in April 1974. Sossi was questioned by his kidnappers for a long period, and the content of his answers, with all its exposures of corruption and malpractices in the judiciary, were then distributed to the press.

Owing to the fact that terrorists needed media and media benefited from terrorists, a strange "love-hate" relationship emerged between them. As RAF formulated it, the media was a "part of capitalist structures." In January 1972 Andreas Baader, one of the first leaders of RAF, wrote a letter to the Deutsche Presse Agentur. In that letter he pointed a finger especially at *Der Spiegel* and Springer Press, claiming, "Every word that for one and half years has been written about us in the pig states' public domain is wrong, is speculation or counterpropaganda." Baader added that the main focus of RAF was "the development of the urban guerilla's propaganda within the revolutionary organizations" (Baader 1972, p.1).

Baader's letter was part of an RAF frontal attack against media. At least once RAF threatened Springer Press with a bomb attack if the press refused to publish the demands of the terrorist organization. Clearly, the other side of this coin was RAF's recognition of the importance of media for its purposes in general and of Springer Press in particular. Joining the chorus, flagship publication of Springer Press, *Der Spiegel*, was often happy to publish RAF material and news about its actions. The best example of such media coverage might be that of the kidnapping of German industrial leader Hanns Martin Schleyer in 1977. This event gained massive publicity. The photo of Schleyer with a placard "Twenty days a prisoner of RAF" with the RAF logo in the background became one of the iconic images in the history of terrorism (Elter 2008).

Parallel to RAF's activities, BR also attacked the press with an accusation that the media was on the wrong side in the class struggle. At the same time BR maintained a certain working relationship with the press. During the kidnapping of former Italian prime minister, Aldo Moro, BR's press releases were central to its publicity campaign to exert pressure on the Italian government to open negotiations and release the group's imprisoned founding members (Monti 2015). As in Germany, when the government refused to negotiate directly with the terrorists, the media served as a forum for indirect negotiations to be held. In this case, the tactic did not help, and the group murdered Moro.

Where the Marxist terrorists found their ethos in leftist scriptures, so did the jihadist in the scriptures of Islam. In both cases propaganda was built on each group's basic ideology. Thus, in order to be reliable propagandists, the representatives of Marxism and jihadism had to sell themselves as authoritative scholars of their ideologies. In this line there are three basic requirements: if you are a scholar you must look like one; you must be fluent in references to your scriptures; and you must find media channel(s) for your message.

Osama bin Laden met those requirements completely. In fact, as a propagandist he had two roles: guerilla leader and Islamic scholar. The two competences were reflected in his dress. In many of his videos and pictures, he wore a camouflage jacket and held a guerrilla "trademark" AK-47 assault rifle. Contrast that attire with his appearance in a 2004 video, when after three years of silence he released an eighteen-minute speech in which he wore a white robe, a golden mantle and a white turban—the uniform of the Islamic "Wise Man of the Mountain." Such a change might have been made to create a contrast between Osama bin Laden and his then-competitor, Abu Musab al-Zarqawi. Al-Zarqawi was originally a militant Islamist from Jordan who was killed on June 7, 2006 by a U.S. Air Force bombing. Al-Zarqawi represented a more violent and militant version of terrorism. He should also be mentioned as an "inventor" of perhaps the most striking and horrific scenes of ISIS propaganda: its ritualistic executions. In the spring of 2004 al-Zarqawi began taking Western hostages. In the summer of the same year an American civilian, Nick Berg, was beheaded by al-Zarqawi with a knife. Berg was dressed in an orange jumpsuit and the executioner wore black balaclavas. The orange jumpsuit was a direct reference to the "uniform" of Guantanamo detainees. The whole performance was videoed and distributed widely (Dyer 2015).

At its early stages Osama bin Laden's propaganda was relatively conventional and was based mainly on videos of his speeches or statements. He was surprisingly successful. He was also able to establish a connection with an important media source, namely, Al Jazeera. Al-Qaeda also produced propaganda to protect his organization against counterterrorist operations. For example, when the headquarters of al-Qaeda was in Khartoum, Sudan, a sharia court led by Ayman al-Zawahiri sentenced two teenage boys to death for treason. Their execution was videoed and disseminated as a warning against any future would-be informants.

The sophistication of al-Qaeda's propaganda increased gradually. In the wake of the Madrid bombings of 2004, one of the operatives, Rabei Osman Sayed Ahmed, was apprehended in Milan, Italy. His propaganda arsenal included three hundred videotapes of jihadist activities in various conflict zones. Moreover, Osama bin Laden also recognized the Internet as a first-class tool to construct the global *ummah*. For that purpose al-Qaeda began running chat rooms such as "The Fortress" (Burleigh 2009). In 2001 al-Qaeda launched a media production arm, As-Sahab Foundation for

Islamic Media Publication, which has released hundreds of videos.

While many elements of ISIS's propaganda were first deployed by al-Qaeda, the propaganda activities of these two terrorist organizations represent two very different concepts. Both in quality and quantity, ISIS raised its activities to a totally different level; it is massive, systematic, formalized, targeted and highly professional. The professionalism is based on two factors: first, ISIS has benefitted from the experiences of other terrorist organizations and Middle Eastern states in conflict, and second, it has been able to enroll professional people from outside its region. ISIS specialists are highly skilled and able to thwart actions that aim to obstruct their presence on the Internet and social media. They have created a network structure that can withstand a siege to ruin its information supply chain (Grzyb, Fahmy, and Shaheen 2015). Moreover, ISIS emphasizes the visual quality of its videos. The executions are often filmed using five to ten cameras and rehearsed a couple of times to select the best angles and scenes. According to journalist and military historian Gwynne Dyer (2015) claims, the videoed death of Canadian foreign fighter André Poulin might even have been staged.

Drawing on a broad international recruiting pool, ISIS has the means to make propaganda in many languages, including some spoken by a relatively small number of people, such as Finnish. In August 2014, for example, Finns were surprised to see a Finnish fighter of Somali origin (his *nom de guerre* was Abu Shu'yab as-Somali) promoting the terrorist organization in fluent Finnish. In addition, a 19-year-old Finn who called himself "Abdullah" became a top propagandist. At its height Abdullah's Twitter account (Mujaahid4Life) had about 11,000 followers whom he fed with a selection of jihadist propaganda videos, images and religious texts. He was considered a "virtual jihadi." According to one source, Abdullah's mother stated that her son came from an atheist family background, he was bullied in school during his younger years and he had no friends and no social life outside of his Internet communications (Williams 2015). In 2013 Abdullah connected with Jabhat al-Nusra supporters who guided him to *Inspire*, al-Qaeda's English-language magazine. As early as the summer of 2013, he was in full swing making al-Nusra propaganda. When al-Nusra and ISIS clashed in the summer of 2014 Abdullah ended up in the ranks of ISIS. Finally, he had found a purpose for his life and felt that he was part of something bigger and important, especially after ISIS declared the Caliphate. In the end, Abdullah started to distance himself from ISIS when the British aid worker Alan Henning was executed in October 2014. Abdullah examined classical Islamic teaching to find justification for the execution, but could not find any. Although his jihadist Twitter account was suspended, he now reportedly uses Twitter to counter ISIS and terrorism (Williams 2015).

In its propaganda ISIS uses material focusing on its combatants and supporters, whereas the leaders are rarely shown. ISIS is systematically building a brand—somewhat like those of international corporations. Mosques may have been the main recruiting venues for al-Qaeda, but for ISIS, according to a defector, 90 percent of its recruits are reached over the Internet (Williams 2015). Some reports in the media clearly indicate that face-to-face social networks and personal contacts are at the center of attempts for recruiting new fighters for ISIS.

The strongest evidence that ISIS has run a successful propaganda campaign is that as many as 30,000 foreign militants have joined its ranks. This is in large part due to how ISIS presents itself. For example, people in the West often refer to ISIS as the "Islamic State" without any hesitation, although both terms, "Islamic" and "state," can be easily challenged on theological and legal grounds. Indeed, ISIS's propaganda is built around the idea that a good image brings power (Benotman and Winter 2015). In order to compete in the scarce market of militants and donors, ISIS has developed an image different from other terrorist organizations. To do so, it has even sacrificed the security of its fighters by publishing material about its frontline activities. By distributing videos and pictures of brutal executions and violence ISIS also tries to sell its own interpretation of justice and wants to send a clear message about the fate of its enemies and apostates. The fact is that ISIS exploits certain Western concepts (such as being a "state") for branding and propaganda purposes. In reality ISIS's actions may rely on a faulty "cherry-picked" interpretation of Islam, but its propaganda creates a vastly different perception in the minds of some: ISIS does not interpret Islam, it is Islam! (Benotman and Winter 2015).

The declaration of the Caliphate in June 2014 made by ISIS

spokesperson Mujahid Sheikh Adnani was a starting point for a heavy propaganda campaign. The title of the declaration was "This is the Promise by Allah." It presents the foundations of the Caliphate and the appointment of Abu Bakr al-Baghdadi, whose birth name was Ibrahim Awwad, as Caliph Ibrahim. Caliph Ibrahim is introduced as a member of al-Qurashi, Prophet Muhammed's tribe. His adopted name, Abu Bakr, refers to the first Caliph after the death of Prophet Muhammed. The declaration also summarizes the Caliphate's future "action program," including the construction of state institutions with governors, sharia courts, an educational system based on *madrasas*, and a taxation system, as well as the demolition of "crosses and graves" and the removal of "the devil."

The declaration states that the foundations of the Caliphate derive from the holy scriptures, traditions and history of Islam. For example, ISIS's goal of victory over superior enemies and rapid expansion is favorably compared to the first twenty-five years of Islam's history. The formation of the Caliphate took place after due consideration by the *Shura* Council of the Islamic State, which claimed that the Islamic State had gained all the elements necessary for the Caliphate, and it would be a sin not to form it. Even the departments of the "state" are named according to the first seventh-century Caliphate. Moreover, it is important to note that the declaration emphasizes that the Caliphate includes Muslims everywhere, not only those in the Islamic State. There is also the promise of Allah: "By Allah, if you disbelieve in democracy, secularism, nationalism, as well as all the other garbage and ideas from the West, and rush to your religion and creed, then by Allah, you will own the earth, and the east and west will submit to you." The promise clearly underlines the antagonism and clash between two sets of values. It is worth mentioning that the declaration was rejected by many Muslim scholars, such as by members of the Sunni Muslim Brotherhood in Syria (al-Adnani 2014; Lund 2014).

ISIS also skillfully employs symbols in its propaganda, and the Caliphate may be the strongest of these symbols. Many nations have their own real or imagined "golden times" and a "cradle" where the nation was born. For the Caliphate, the Raqqa-Mosul region is the mythical birthplace for the new Caliphate. Selling the Caliphate as an ideal society and utopia becomes easier since the main target audience consists of converts and second-

or third-generation Muslim immigrants in Western countries whose knowledge of the teachings and history of Islam is limited. A study by Anita Perešin (2015) shows that the women who left European countries to join ISIS often claimed that religion was their main motivation. Some of them recounted that they had listened to al-Baghdadi's call to join the ranks of ISIS, and they perceived their support of the Caliphate as their religious duty. Moreover, they stressed that by joining ISIS they felt able to participate in building a new and better society in contrast to the morally corrupted West.

ISIS's worldview not only competes with Western values but also with ancient Eastern ones. This battle line has been delineated by the destruction of archaeological sites and museums. In the Mosul museum the ancient statues were crushed as "false idols" and extensive parts of the old capital of the Assyrian empire Nimrud were destroyed. UNESCO called this latter action a "war crime." ISIS also totally destroyed the oldest monastery in Iraq, St. Elijah's Church, built around 1,400 years ago (Moore 2016). Likewise, ISIS's temporary conquest of Palmyra, the center of a great ancient empire, was marked by raising the black ISIS flag on the citadel above the city. In a way, ISIS assumed dominance over the past and the values and religions of others.

The main aim of ISIS's propaganda is to promote the expansion of the state or Caliphate. This aim requires four different lines of effort: to support, to unite, to frighten and to inform. ISIS has obviously understood that success is the most effective propaganda tool, as the relative share of the last line of effort—informing about events on the ground—has considerably increased with territorial expansion since 2014 (Grzyb, Fahmy, and Shaheen 2015).

ISIS needs fighters and women in order to expand the state and the Caliphate they created. It uses videos, photo reports and Internet magazines to create an atmosphere for their recruitment efforts. It has used several social media platforms, such as Twitter, Facebook and Instagram, and in this realm ISIS relies on more tailored and directed propaganda, which in turn can have a network effect. Although individuals have diverse reasons and motivations for joining ISIS, a preliminary Finnish report based on interviews with friends and relatives of those who have joined ISIS stresses the important role networking plays: out of eighteen people who joined, fifteen of them had formed a connection with one another—the other three were not members of the network but lone wolves who had departed to join ISIS before the others (Creutz, Saarinen, and Juntunen 2015).

Anita Perešin's (2015) study stresses the importance of direct propaganda using social media. According to her findings, approximately 550 Muslim girls and women from the West have joined ISIS. They are usually sixteen to twenty-five years old, some even younger. Many of them are educated with a solid family background as second- or third-generation immigrants in the West, and in most cases the family objected to their plan to travel to the conflict area.

As there is always a combination of motivations for joining a group like ISIS, it is difficult to rank them in any order. Teenage girls and young women offer three main reasons for joining ISIS: adventure, religion, and the chance to become the wife of a holy warrior and give birth to the next generation of warriors. Many believed becoming a member of ISIS/ the Caliphate was their religious duty, as al-Baghdadi has declared. Perešin (2015) informs us that ISIS is aware of these motivations and has developed its propaganda strategy accordingly. For example, ISIS's operation for recruiting women is run by women who themselves have gone through the same experience. As a result, ISIS recruiters can maintain a cozy woman-to-woman atmosphere in their communication with possible recruits. They know targeted females' attractions and main concerns. They can talk about the travel arrangements, clothing needs, and daily life in the Islamic State. Regarding primary concerns, they can openly tell the possible recruits how difficult it is to face family opposition to their plan to join ISIS, and how to deal with this obstacle. In brief, it is a totally new type of social media campaign where the women working for ISIS create a kind of ground-level subnarrative derived from the organization's grand Islamic Caliphate narrative (Perešin 2015).

Systematic propaganda does not end when the new recruits, male or female, arrive in the Islamic State. They usually have to undergo a six-week-long training. ISIS defectors interviewed by Anne Speckhard and Ahmet S. Yayla (Speckhard and Yayla 2015) present the following picture: the main part of the training program is of a military nature, but there is also a strong

Islamic indoctrination element. This is totally in line with other ideology-based military organizations (for example, Waffen-SS and the Soviet Red Army), even though these military organizations' ideologies do not focus on religion. A ten-day sharia training is run by well-educated, charismatic and convincing teachers. The starting point of the religious teaching is that ISIS has the only right interpretation of Islam, the "true Islam," based on Wahhabism or Salafism. By extension, this makes other types of Muslims apostates and legitimate targets for killing.

8

HOMEGROWN TERRORISTS

When an individual shoots and kills another person we say that he or she committed homicide. In most cases homicide victims are those who were known by the murderer, and usually there are tragic personal motivations for committing homicide. Criminologists differentiate between homicide and mass murder. Mass murder involves the killing of four or more people by one or multiple assailants within a single event. One version of mass murder is known as spree killing, in which a killer commits murder in two or more locations with virtually no break in between. Another category is serial killing. In this case the killer murders three or more individuals with a cooling-off period between each one. It is an accepted fact that most serial killers prefer other methods for murdering their victims than shooting because, for psychological reasons, they wish to observe their victims' suffering.

When criminologists talk about multiple homicides, such as those directed by Charles Manson in 1969, they exclude highly organized or institutionalized murders such as war crimes, political terrorism or certain acts committed by crime rings and gangs. According to criminal justice scholars James Alan Fox and Jack Levin, highly organized or institutional murders "may be better explained through the theories and methods of political science than criminology" (Fox and Levin 2003, p. 47).

In this book we already looked at psychodynamic explanations for why people kill in the name of large-group identity, ethnicity, religion or ideology. Such a murderer is often a member of an organizing group. In such cases, the murderer is referred to as a "terrorist" and is an agent of a strong spillover of terrorism. On other occasions, when someone acts in the name of large-group identity without being a member of an organization or institution, the murderer is called a "homegrown terrorist" (Olsson 2014) and is an agent of a weak spillover of terrorism. In this chapter we will focus on those killers of innocent people who wear the cloak of a religious or ideological large-group identity and are receivers of malignant propaganda, but who are not trained by a terrorist organization. J. Reid Meloy and Jessica Yakeley (2014) reviewed the existing research on lone-wolf terrorists and offered psychoanalytic understanding of these terrorists' minds. They state that such individuals exhibit certain characteristics such as personal grievance, moral outrage, disillusionment with the social order around them, narcissistic wounds, failure of sexual pair bonding, sexualization of violence, dependence on virtual communication on the Internet, radicalization fueled by changes in thinking and emotion and predatory violence allowed by their superegos. Meloy and Yakeley's work led them to postulate that a pathologically narcissistic self-structure in which primitive modes of thinking predominate exists at the foundation of a lone wolf's mind. They tell us, however, that the violent true believer is not a homogenous type. We agree with this opinion.

Another psychoanalyst who studied homegrown terrorists is Peter Olsson (2014). His samples of such persons in the United States include believers in various religions. He too noted psychodynamic patterns in the homegrown terrorists he studied. Such patterns include severe ambivalence or disappointment in early parental figures, difficulties in passing through the adolescence passage and prolonged adolescent identity searching, ambivalence about a spouse and intimacy, fear or hatred of authority, narcissistic injury and radicalization by reading and memorizing the Quran, the Bible, or another ideological book. Olsson's and Meloy and Yakeley's findings, we noted, support one another.

Here we will provide one example of a homegrown terrorist who was a highly educated Jewish man. We do not have knowledge of his childhood and we cannot make a psychological formulation about his mind. Benjamin Goldstein (later to be known as Baruch Goldstein) was born in the United States in 1956. He was a graduate of Albert Einstein College of Medicine in New York and immigrated to Israel in 1983. He was a follower of Rabbi Meir Kahane, who had evolved a political, ideological and religious movement known as Kahanism. Kahanism focused on adopting *halakha* (Jewish law) in public life in Israel, limiting Israeli citizenship to Jews only, forcibly evicting all Arab Muslims from Israeli-controlled lands and annexing the Biblical land of Israel. Kahane openly supported the use of terror against Arabs. Kahane founded *Kach,* a political party, in Israel. In 1988, his party was declared "racist" and banned by the Knesset. Two years later Kahane was assassinated in New York by El Sayyid Nosair, an Egyptian Muslim who, obviously, also killed in the name of religion.

Baruch Goldstein, the physician, was a charter member of the Jewish Defense League (JDL). After migrating to Israel, he served in the military and then lived in the Kiryat Arba settlement near Hebron. The southern bank of Hebron is the location where the historic "Cave of Patriarchs" is located. According to Jewish tradition, the tombs of Prophet Abraham and his family members are located in this cave. On top of this cave stands Ibrahimi Mosque (Mosque of Abraham), which has been there since 1206. But the Cave of Patriarchs also includes a section for the Jews to worship. At this historical place symbolic mental representations of two religions stand next to each other in a concrete way. There are rules and customs for worshipping at this location. For example, for ten days each year the entire cave is utilized by Jews, and on another ten days Muslims are allowed to use the entire place.

Muslim and Jewish religious holidays appear at different times in different years on a Gregorian calendar, which means they sometimes occur simultaneously. Under these circumstances, the shared nature of the cave presents potential problems since religious or ethnic large groups, like other large groups, become anxious when a psychological border is not maintained, including the symbols that represent them. This is what happened when the Muslim holiday of Ramadan and the Jewish holiday Purim overlapped in February 1994. As Muslims arrived for evening prayers on Thursday, February 24, Jewish settlers from Kiryat Arba and Israeli soldiers on duty at the Cave of the Patriarchs prevented Muslim Palestinians from entering. Although they were eventually allowed in with the stipulation that they leave by 10:00 p.m., which they did, Israeli settlers set off fireworks in their direction as they did so, creating a general atmosphere of tension. The Purim eve celebrations too were disrupted by a group of Palestinian youths chanting "*Itbah al- Yahud*" (slaughter the Jews). Dr. Baruch Goldstein attended the Purim service that evening.

Early the next morning Muslim worshippers in the Ibrahimi Mosque were kneeling and prostrating before Allah, when gunshots rang out. The shooter was Goldstein, dressed in his old army uniform, firing an IMI Galil assault rifle. Twenty-nine Muslims were killed and over one hundred more were wounded. The crowd subdued him with a fire extinguisher and then beat him to death.

Some right-wing fundamentalist Jews consider Baruch Goldstein a martyr, despite his terrible crime. His burial site at Kiryat Arba, in a park that carries the name of Rabbi Kahane, became a small shrine. Written on his tombstone are the words: "Here lies the saint, Dr. Baruch Kappel Goldstein, blessed be the memory of the righteous and holy man, may the Lord avenge his blood, who devoted his soul to the Jews, Jewish religion and Jewish land. His hands are innocent and his heart is pure. He was killed as a martyr of God on the 14th of Adar, Purim, in the year 5754 [1994]."

The shrine was dismantled in 2000, a few years after the Knesset passed a bill on order from the High Court of Israel forbidding the erection of monuments to those who are considered "terrorists"—although some right-wing Baruch Goldstein followers objected. The inscription, however, still remains on Goldstein's tombstone.

In trying to make sense of this horrible event and the concept of killing in the name of one's God, we presume that Baruch Goldstein and others like him must have personal issues that intertwined with the influence of large-group psychology. Arych Kizel, in the March 1, 1994 issue of *Yedioth Ahronoth*, maintained that Baruch Goldstein was threatened with court-martial when serving in the Israeli Army because he refused medical care to all non-Jews. Although we cannot confirm this information, we do know that failure to be accepted increases isolation. Such histories have been found in other homegrown terrorists' lives (Meloy and Yakeley 2014; Olsson 2014; Puckett 2001).

We can guess that before he committed the murders Baruch Goldstein had personal reasons for separating himself from nonbelievers and even destroying them in order to maintain this separateness. It can be said that his ideas were very close to the ideas of radical Muslims. Indeed, people who are followers of radical fundamentalist religious thinking share similarities in spite of their belonging to different religions. In that sense, Goldstein's mind reflected the thinking of hundreds of thousands of others who belong to an extreme religious organization, whether the organization is linked to Judaism or Christianity or Islam.

Within the past decade, homegrown Muslim jihadist terrorists have committed attacks in Belgium, Denmark, England, France, Spain, Sweden, Turkey, the United States, and elsewhere. Certain psychological and social factors may indirectly play a role in the emergence of homegrown terrorists in the West. For example, Europe is facing a huge refugee crisis. The unprecedented surge of migrants and refugees flooding into Europe threatens the stability of host countries' psychological large-group identity borders (Volkan 2017). Even in the United States, attempts are being made to restrict the entry of Muslims from certain countries. Such negative attitudes and policies can become a factor in isolating a newcomer and leading him or her to hold on to terrorist organizations' malignant propaganda as psychological food.

Ultra-right, populist and anti-immigration parties have gained strength in many European countries. For example, an opinion poll in Finland shows that 30 percent of city and community councilors are not ready to accept the new Finns as Finns, even if they have citizenship, speak Finnish and come from families who have already lived in Finland for many generations (*Kaleva* newspaper, 6 December, 2015). Immigrants face racism, discrimination and even hate crimes, but on the other hand "natives" face "ordinary" crimes and also terrorist attacks committed by immigrants—potentially establishing a self-perpetuating cycle of violence. Jeff Victoroff, Janice R. Adelman and Miriam Matthews (2012) have written about how contacts between individuals in diaspora communities and individuals in their countries of origin can serve as a "conveyor belt" of terrorist propaganda. They state that both actual and perceived discrimination may be the main factor affecting the minds of those living in Muslim diaspora communities.

To explore further how a homegrown terrorist can kill other innocent humans whom he or she does not know, including children, for religion or ideology we need to examine one more concept: dehumanization. The concept of dehumanization needs to be examined not only in order to understand how a homegrown terrorist's superego gives him or her permission to kill, but also to expand our insight into suicide bombings and other murders and even genocides performed in the service of separating perpetrators' large-group identity from the unwanted identity of victims.

In an informal exchange between Anna Freud and the late, well-known psychoanalyst Joseph Sandler, the former said, "We know that with persecuted minorities, against whom atrocities are committed, the atrocities are preceded by a withdrawal of the feeling of sameness [by the victimizer]" (Sandler and Freud 1983, p. 6). Anna Freud identified this action as a version of dehumanization and added that "without this preliminary withdrawal or boundary setting what happens afterwards could not happen, because of the feeling of sympathy and empathy, of sameness, which has to be done away with" (p. 67). Psychoanalyst Ira Brenner, who has extensively studied Holocaust survivors' trauma (2014), describes dehumanization in a moving way by referring to the plight of children during the Holocaust (2016), a topic that was largely overlooked for decades, the well-known fate of Anne Frank notwithstanding. He reminds us that approximately 1.5 million Jewish children were murdered during the Holocaust—roughly 89 percent of those alive in Europe in 1939 (Dwork 1991). Brenner states that if one thinks of the challenges confronting an exterminator who tries to rid a property of vermin, then such an unbelievable tragedy becomes more comprehensible. He adds: "After all, what could be more effective than destroying nests, eggs, larvae, newly hatched offspring and pregnant females?" Nazi propaganda is full of examples of dehumanization. In Rwanda, Hutus first referred to Tutsis as evil, and later began calling them *cafards*, meaning cockroaches. Dehumanization has also been examined by other psychoanalysts (Akhtar

2009; Bernard, Ottenberg and Redl 1973; Volkan 1988, 1997, 2013).

A homegrown terrorist (or suicide bomber) utilizes *strategy-based* dehumanization (Akhtar 2009). Such a killer perceives the victim more and more as a stereotype of negative qualities. Dehumanizing people comes close to "experiencing their enemy as the original nonhuman or inanimate suitable target of externalization of their childhood, which had become a reservoir for shared all-bad parts and their accompanying affect" (Volkan 1988, p. 120). Dehumanization helps the murderer avoid experiencing guilt or remorse. Hurting or killing "cockroaches" does not induce the guilt feelings that hurting other human beings would. The late, well-known Israeli psychoanalyst Rafael Moses (1981) reminded us that the murderer of the Other loses his or her own humanity in dehumanizing another; were it not lost, such savage behavior as then occurs would not be possible. However, a terrorist denies this loss of humanity. Furthermore, getting rid of the enemy results in absolute differentiation from the enemy and causes the aggressor's collective bad aspects to disappear with the dead enemy, thereby prohibiting a boomerang effect (Volkan 1997). In short, what was projected and externalized onto the Other would not be reinternalized because of the death of the Other. If the terrorist commits suicide during the terrorist attack, this person never even has to face the boomerang effect. In psychological terms, a suicide bomber never deals with the difficulty of externalization-reinternalization of unwanted "bad" thoughts and affects.

9

WITH GOD ON OUR SIDE

Ideological and Economic Perspectives

In public life killing the Other brings the concept of morality to our attention. We have the moral faculty to judge right and wrong. Marc Hauser, an evolutionary biologist (2009) who has done research in the field of animal and human cognition, calls it "our universal moral grammar." He claims that possessing moral judgment is universal since, in a general sense, it is immune to cultural variation. Hauser's proposition for a universal moral grammar does not describe in detail the moral process or mechanism leading, for example, to making a decision not to kill in one particular situation and to consider it the right thing to do in another. Nevertheless, it is a positive thing that we are able to evaluate our actions.

All the major religions of the world have taken positions concerning killing. Although there are several approaches, the main line, more or less clearly, is to prohibit killing. In Judaism and Christianity killing is expressly forbidden: "Thou shalt not kill" (the Fifth Commandment). Yet, God can obviously break his own commandments and even order his people to commit genocide. According to Deuteronomy 20:17, God commanded the death of six separate peoples at once. In Islam it is indicated that when there is a just cause, killing can take place. In Surah 6:151 it is stated: "...

and kill not anyone whom Allah has forbidden, except for a just cause." Buddhism asks only to avoid killing. We should not forget that leaders and authorities of religious terrorist organizations have their own versions and interpretations of religion.

Historian Yuval Noah Harari states that religion is "a system of human norms and values that is founded on a belief in a superhuman order." He continues: "Based on this superhuman order, religion establishes norms and values that it considers binding" (2014, p. 234). Almost without exception every religion has been exploited to support a high standard of moral behavior. Yet, every religion also has been hijacked for utmost cruelty and killing. Humans kill in the name of God, while thinking or believing that God is on their side. When God is on the killer's side, this helps and supports killing the Other. There must be a rational explanation for such irrational behavior of gods, and throughout history humans have been searching for answers from the gods themselves. As a consequence, there has been circular reasoning: we behave in a certain way because we think it is what gods want us to do.

During the last part of the twentieth century, a worldwide increase in investment in religion took place. Let us look at Islam first. In 1979 there was the Islamic revolution in Iran, which led to the emergence of a theocratic Shi'ite state. Parallel to this development, Saudi Arabia started to build up its position as the leader of Sunni Islam by supporting and financing the spreading of its own version of Sunnism, Wahhabism or Salafism. Consequently, there was now a new competition between conservative versions of Sunni and Shia Islam. While both versions are held regionally, there are attempts to spread them to other locations.

Similar changes have occurred within the world of Christianity. The most significant of these took place in the balance between the different denominations inside Christianity and in the spread of charismatic and transdenominational Christianity, particularly Pentecostalism and evangelical Protestantism. The global south, mostly composed of developing countries in the Southern hemisphere, South and Central America and sub-Saharan Africa, has been noted as the site of the most dramatic religious explosion in the world today (Thomas 2010). Pentecostalism and evangelical Protestantism have been traditionally considered highly personalized belief systems. The believers' focus had been on their individualized relationship with their God, not on politics. Lately, Pentecostalism and evangelical Protestantism have become associated with political movements more and more, especially in South America. In this region these denominations usually support democracy and religious freedom. Yet, as they represent "biblical literalism," they also catalyze intolerance. Promoting Christianity in developing countries leads to a problem, a clash between Christianity and other traditional religions, including Islam. As Christianity becomes the dominant religion and is radicalized, it may also create fruitful soil for Christian terrorism (Thomas 2010).

Olivier Roy (2010), a French political scientist, in his book *Holy Ignorance: When Religion and Culture Part Ways*, has examined the relations between three religious movements—Salafism, Pentecostalism and evangelical Protestantism—and their influence on societies' culture and politics. Roy claims that these three religious groups have become universal after spreading to foreign territories and after being removed from their cultural roots and connections. It became easier for people in these territories to use these religious movements in the political arena, applying various strategies for purposes ranging from democratic to terroristic. According to Roy, globalization has weakened local cultures. In turn, fundamentalist versions of religions have increased and led to, as the title of his book suggests, "Holy Ignorance." However, historian and sociologist Karen Barkey (2011) criticized Roy's views. According to her, local cultures are not weakening; they even have been revitalized by globalization. She stresses that religion in new territories is not inherited but chosen and as a result the arrival of new religious movements has not replaced local cultures, but more likely, the new religion has become a part of the old local culture. Barkey's opinion finds support in the case of Finland, but Finland's situation is somewhat different from what's happening elsewhere today. The Pentecostal Church reached Finland a hundred years ago, not as a recent globalization activity. At the moment it has about 50,000 members, and it appears that the members of the Church are culturally as much Finnish as other Finns who have been following the teaching of another Protestant Christian Church, the Lutheran Protestant Church, for almost five hundred years. A vast majority, 73 percent of

Finns, are members of the Lutheran Protestant Church.

This new increased investment in religion has inevitably had certain negative effects. Since the 1960s, all major religions of the world have been connected to terrorism. As mentioned, radical Jewish nationalists have committed acts of terror, as have Christians. In Northern Ireland, for example, violent conflict occurred for years between the Irish Republican Army (IRA)—"Catholics" and sometimes even Marxists—and the Ulster Volunteer Force or Ulster Defense Association—"Protestants" and loyalists in favor of keeping Northern Ireland as part of England. In the United States, God's Army, a Christian faith-based terrorist organization, has staged over a hundred attacks, mainly against abortion clinics. The Ugandan Lord's Resistance Army has committed horrendous acts, and Oklahoma City bomber Timothy McVeigh had connections with certain movements—the Christian Identity Movement and the Covenant, the Sword and the Arm of the Lord—that favored a Christian theocratic government in the United States.

At least two cases of terrorism and violence related to Buddhism are worth mentioning. A Buddhist-inspired cult, Aum Shinrikyo, founded in 1984 by Shoko Asahara released the chemical weapon sarin in the Tokyo subway in 1995, killing thirteen individuals, severely injuring about 50 others and affecting hundreds more. In Myanmar, the Muslim Rohingya minority has lately been the target of Buddhist terror, even genocide, while extremist Hindu nationalist groups have similarly targeted minority Muslim communities in India.

In this book we have already made multiple references to the intersection of radical Islam and terrorism. Instead of recounting the list of such terrorist attacks here, we will describe one *anticipated* incident of mass violence—not a terrorist attack, but a battle. As ISIS's propaganda machinery has made known, ISIS expected a prophetic battle between good and evil to take place in Dabiq, near Aleppo, in Syria. In an article in *The Atlantic*, Canadian journalist Graeme Wood (2015) detailed how ISIS's propagandists drooled with anticipation of this event. The belief in such an upcoming battle is similar to the perception of the battle of Armageddon in Judaism and Christianity. Although Dabiq is no longer under ISIS control, Wood correctly noted that somehow Western media frequently missed references to Dabiq in ISIS videos and has not focused on the importance of ISIS's preoccupation with the apocalypse. A strong belief in a forthcoming apocalypse most likely plays a role in recruiting people to ISIS and training some of them as suicide bombers. More recently, ISIS has turned its attention to Rome as both a symbolic and military target, as reflected in the rebranding of its online publication from *Dabiq* to *Rumiyah* (Arabic for Rome).

We find a belief in apocalypse not only in religious ideology, but also in Marxist secular ideology. In the fight song of the proletariat, "The Internationale," there is reference to a "final battle." It appears that both Marxism and jihadism would like to create a new world through destruction of the existing one. In Marxism, before the final battle the existing world is divided into two spheres: the sphere of communism (that is the sphere of peace) and the sphere of capitalism (that is the sphere of war, or at least exploitation). Islam has a similar division: *dar ul-islam* (the abode of peace) and *dar ul-harb* (abode of war). The representative of the new political order in Marxism is the proletariat state, which will transform itself to a communist state and establish, in the end, a global communist entity. In Islam it is the Caliphate that will establish a global *umma*, whereby the whole world has been converted to Islam. In political Islam both the Caliphate and global *umma* are based on theocracy; in Marxism order is based on the dictatorship of the proletariat. They also both aim to create cleansed entities, politically or religiously. Therefore, we can say that the final goals of both Marxists and jihadists are entirely secular or "earthly": after establishing a state based on their ideology, they would proceed toward global governance. For both the final aim is all about power here on Earth.

Political scientist Heather Selma Gregg (2014) states that religiously motivated terrorism includes traits of secular terrorism. Reading Gregg's work has rekindled Jouni Suistola's own memories from the late 1960s and early 1970s when "a specter was once again haunting Europe—the specter of Communism." At that time it was connected with the radicalization of students, which created the leftist "bulge" described earlier. In some European countries the bulge formed the platform for Marxist terrorism. Fortunately, in Finland it did not go so far. At that time Suistola and other non-Marxist Finnish students were continuously exposed to the "fact" that the Marxists represented the eternal truth and that all students like Suistola represented bourgeoisie nonsense. The opposition was fluent with citations from Marx, Engels and Lenin, which they had learned directly from their "holy scriptures," called Marxist-Leninist study circles. Much later, when Suistola read jihadist scriptures, he experienced a feeling of déjà vu. Now, the only difference was the presentation of jihadism as the only "right ideology," instead of Marxism.

Gregg (2014) also writes about the importance of examining the *differences* between religiously motivated terrorism and secular ideologically motivated terrorism. She refers to the work of scholars such as Mark Juergensmayer, Walter Laqueur and Bruce Hoffman, which supports the idea that the difference between the two types of terrorism is that religious terrorism is marked with extreme violence, brutality, irrational motivations and goals. Gregg reminds us of how Walter Laqueur saw religious terrorism as the new terrorism of the right. However, according to her, Laqueur's definition cannot explain organizations like Aum Shinrikyo in Japan. Gregg refers to another scholar, this time to David C. Rapoport, and tells us that religious terrorism uses both historic examples and sacred texts. For example, al-Qaeda has referred to Western countries "Crusaders," and ISIS has adapted the term Caliphate. Finally, Gregg refers to Mark Sedgwick, who proposed that the difference between two types of terrorism lies in immediate and ultimate objectives. Gregg herself comes up with the following definition of religiously motivated terrorism: "The threat or use of force with the purpose of influencing or coercing governments and/ or populations towards saliently religious goals" (2014, p. 39) and picks up the three main goals of religious terrorism: apocalypse, theocracy and religious cleansing.

In apocalyptic terrorism the goal of the terrorist group is to cause massive destruction to property and people in order to speed up the coming of the end of time and the consequent utopia. For Gregg "this pursuit is uniquely religious" (p. 39). As examples of such terrorist groups she mentions Gush Emunim in Israel and Aum Shinrikyo in Japan. Gush Emunim aimed for the destruction of the Dome of the Rock at the Temple Mount, Jerusalem, with the hope of triggering confrontation between Israel and Arab states with the use of weapons of mass destruction. Aum

Shinrikyo launched a Sarin nerve gas attack in the Tokyo subway.

Religious cleansing is a form of ethnic cleansing, where ethnicity is narrowly defined by religion only. Both religious and ethnic cleansing is contaminated with the concept of large-group identity. Religious cleansing has especially been the goal of ISIS. It is estimated that about 5,000 Yazidi men have been killed and almost the same number of Yazidi women have been abducted. In September 2015 there were some signs that ISIS was going to allow at least some Christians and Muslim "apostates" to live inside its territory, although under strict rules. Unlike what ISIS has done, at the present time there is no religious cleansing under internationally recognized Islamic governments; other sects of Islam or religions can exist in Islamic countries, but often under difficult conditions. In Iran, for example, there are about 300,000 Jews and roughly the same number of Christians and Baha'is. Radical religious groups have a tendency to make life miserable not only for the representatives of other religions and sects, but also for all the people who do not share their radical religious beliefs and practices.

Even in today's Turkey, a member of NATO and legally a secular state, citizens who have a different religious belief system than those who are followers of the governing religious party, AK Parti (AKP), are facing a kind of "soul murder." Leonard Shengold (1991) originally used the term "soul murder" to refer to the abuse or neglect of children that deprives them of their identity and ability to experience joy in life. Here we use this term to illustrate how an authoritarian political leader or regime fills many citizens' lives with helplessness and fear and interferes with or even ruins their enjoyment of daily activities. Their ability to assert themselves is lost. This situation leads to fragmentation within the society between those who are followers of the authoritarian political leader and those who suffer from "soul murder." For over a decade AKP leadership has been trying to change the large-group identity of the Turkish Republic, which was founded in 1923 under the leadership of Kemal Atatürk following the collapse of the Ottoman Empire, to make the country more religious and to erode Turkey's secular traditions. Vamık Volkan (2013) gave examples from the mid-2000s illustrating such efforts. His examples included news about more than one million children "volunteering" to take Quran lessons, distribution of a picture of Spider-Man flying on a prayer rug to youngsters, public discussions on the destruction of statues of men or women showing nakedness and forbidding female medical students from examining male patients. Thousands of new mosques have been constructed. The idea that the required religious custom of washing one's hands, feet and face before prayer would increase red blood cells and make one resistant to illness was publicized. Such examples have multiplied since the mid-2000s. In May 2013, a religious school student received first prize at a national science fair run by the Scientific and Technological Research Council of Turkey's (TÜBİTAK). He "proved" that reading the Quran to a common bean grown will cause it to grow three times faster than normal beans. TÜBİTAK is an advisory agency to the Turkish government. Meanwhile, women who do not marry and have children have been declared as "half human beings." In July 2016, Vamık Volkan gave a public lecture in Istanbul during which references to Sigmund Freud were made. That evening he watched on television as an AKP politician advocated for removing the names of Sigmund Freud and Charles Darwin from Turkish school books. When Vamık Volkan spoke with a very high-level government official in Turkey a few years earlier, this gentleman appeared to have a genuine belief that the AKP had succeeded in creating a new Turkish large-group identity, dismissing the existence of the section of the population who were experiencing "soul murder."

Another dimension of this changing Turkish identity has involved the so-called Gülen movement. Fethullah Gülen, a former imam, has been living as an exile in the United States since 1999. He has opened hundreds of charter schools in many countries, including the United States. His so-called "mild" religious teachings may have been welcomed by U.S. officials because they saw his message as a counter to "violent" Islam. Although we have no evidence of this possibility and no information from where the Gülen movement has received financial backing, Gülen had a mission for changing the Turkish Republic. In a sermon Gülen gave in 1999 (Turkish channel ATV, June 18, 1999), he described the Republic of Turkey as "a nation that has accepted atheism" and run away from itself. Without using bullets and bombs he wanted Turkey "to come back riding on its horse."

Before 2013 Gülen was an ally of Recep Tayyip Erdoğan, the current president of Turkey and the leader of the AKP. Gülen's followers infiltrated into the Turkish police force, military, legal and educational establishments. A struggle between two so-called "mild" Islamic movements unfolded. Gülen's followers in Turkey made a coup attempt on July 15, 2016, while the society was still in a state of fear following the ISIS terrorist attack at Istanbul Atatürk Airport on June 29. The coup attempt failed, but more than 240 people died and some 1,500 persons were wounded during the attempt. Gülen has to date denied any involvement in this tragedy, as the Turkish government continues to ask the U.S. government to send Gülen back to Turkey to face criminal charges.

Within a matter of days after the coup attempt, government officials came up with the names of more than 60,000 individuals—military personnel, judges, academicians, students, members of the media—who would be arrested, fired, suspended or questioned by the police. All of Gülen's "viruses" would be removed. It can easily be assumed that this list existed before July 15. Many schools, hospitals and think tanks were quickly closed and travel restrictions were placed on academicians. While thousands of persons celebrated in the streets with flags and references to "Allah," who was credited with preventing the coup, innocent individuals suffering from "soul murder" began experiencing a new wave of fear with the possibility that they may be wrongly punished. They became scared of the possibility of "secularism cleansing." We will wait to see whether there will be a positive outcome to the present situation in Turkey or whether more tragedies will follow.

Unlike the situation in a secular ideological terrorist group, a leader of a religious terrorist organization bases his authority on religion. This authority can be self-proclaimed when the leader is not a religious scholar. Osama bin Laden, Ayman al- Zawahiri and Shoko Asahara made such claims. Then there are leaders with "proper" religious credentials, such as Sheikh Yassin of Hamas, Sheikh Fadlallah of Hezbollah and Rabbi Meir Kahane of the Jewish Defense League (JDL). Abu Bakr al-Baghdadi claims he received a PhD from the Islamic University of Baghdad.

What of the claim that Marxism is another "religious" ideology, just like jihadism?

One major difference between Marxist ideology and jihadism rests in their respective time perspectives. The Marxists' aim was and still is to be involved in a progressive move (even though there is a reference to a "final battle" in their international song) and to create something in the future, a utopia that has yet to exist. On the other hand, the jihadist movement is regressive. Its aim is to re-create something that existed a long time ago: during the Golden Times of the early Islamic Caliphate with a pure (that is radical conservative) interpretation of Islam. After the Apocalypse there will be a world as it existed in Golden Times. Marx was never able to characterize in detail the essence of a communist state. The jihadists face a similar problem: their longed-for Golden Times never existed.

In order to shed more light on radical religious and terrorist organizations we will now look at the relations between religion and economics. Economist Laurence Iannaccone, who notes that during the last decades instead of a more secularized world we have seen the rise of a more religious world, informs us that "virtually every measure of religious involvement or commitment correlates positively with the denomination's overall level of conservatism, strictness, or sectarianism" (1998 p. 1472). Liberal Protestants in the United States contribute around 1.5 percent of their income to their church, whereas Mormons contribute 6 percent. Iannaccone explains that a religious group functions as a "mutual-benefit organization" where the members "contribute both to production and consumption of … religious commodities" (p. 1482). The so-called free riders drop out.

There is the question of why the members of religious groups are ready for considerable personal sacrifice for the benefit of the religious organization, even in circumstances where such an organization often purposely restricts the opportunities for the members to access secular activities and rewards. Following Laurence Iannaccone, economist Eli Berman (2009) deals with this question. While rejecting the view that religion itself makes the religious terrorist organizations so deadly, Berman informs us that the leaders of the most lethal terrorist groups have found a way to control defection. He refers to a Viet Minh veteran who stated that if somebody in the group was killed, it took a few days for the organization to recover, but it took weeks or months if somebody defected from the group.

To be able to prove trustworthiness, the member must make sacrifices. To recruit new members and to keep the old ones the group must offer sufficient compensation. The result is a "competition" between sacrifices and compensation. Successful terrorist organizations meet the spiritual needs of their members and provide social, health and educational services for them. Berman gives an example of such a condition existing even within a religious organization that is not a terrorist one. Sixty percent of ultra-Orthodox Jewish men in Israel are not working or looking for a job, but studying in yeshivas with a poor return of their "investment" in terms of future job opportunities or higher salaries.

Terrorist organizations offer a new purpose in life and the illusion of serving a highly important cause. This takes place while the organization demands sacrifices from its members. The members' sacrifices include their staying with the organization and not defecting; remaining as members becomes an investment for their lifetime. Cheaters and "free riders" are eliminated. Meanwhile, the members of the group must follow certain ritualistic practices that are sometimes time consuming. This makes the members different from those in the mainstream culture. Very often the organization also imposes a strict clothing code, such as special headgear to strengthen the group's identity. Such organizations also introduce strict and exceptional behavioral norms, such as banning alcohol, movies, television, beaches and coffee shops and declaring men must have a long beard. Sometimes, the social contacts are allowed only inside the group. Berman (2009) reminds us that the better services the organization offers, the stricter the rules it can impose. He also reminds us that very often the organization also introduces rules for sexual relations, or even organizes those activities through the group. It is no wonder that ISIS has emphasized the importance of recruiting girls for their fighters and even justified the use of sex slaves and repeated gang rapes of girls and women in occupied areas. Here it follows the rule that the more the organization offers, the more lethal it usually is. ISIS's cruel treatment of local populations is connected with its attempt to limit contacts with the locals and minimize defection (Berman 2009). It has also been cruel toward its own members if they have behaved in a suspicious way: the internal police force of ISIS has executed dozens of its fighters as "traitors" or "spies." Yet, if an organization does not keep its promises and live up to its teaching, there will always be defectors.

Peter Neumann (2015) published a report on fifty-eight ISIS members from seventeen countries (including twenty-one Syrians) who defected between January 2014 and August 2015. Neumann found the following: the defectors stated that they had joined ISIS to satisfy a desire to help other Muslims, to fight for a holy cause and to have an opportunity to become heroes. The defectors from Syria also wanted to escape the atrocities of the Assad government. But, all were attracted to the terrorist organization also because of promises of luxury goods, cars and adventures. Their reasons for defecting included brutality and atrocities carried out against other Muslims and the corruption and un-Islamic nature of ISIS. They declared that life under ISIS had been harsh and disappointing for them.

10

RESTRICTED EXTREME RELIGIOUS FUNDAMENTALISM

In 1901, Sigmund Freud rewrote the well-known text of Genesis, "God created man in His own image," as "Man created God in his" (p. 19). According to him, the terrifying impressions of helplessness in childhood and the duration of one's sense of helplessness—overt or covert—throughout life make it necessary to seek an omnipotent father, an image of God, to assuage the feeling of vulnerability. Thus, religion is related to shared illusion (Freud 1927, 1930). After noticing a close similarity between obsessive acts and religious practices, he viewed obsessional neurosis as a distorted private religion, and religion as a kind of universal obsessional neurosis. For a very long time after Freud, few psychoanalysts dealt with the topic of religion or seriously questioned Freud's assumptions in any depth. As expected, "animosity" between religion and psychoanalysis evolved, and psychoanalysts in general ignored the topic. In 1953 a British pediatrician and psychoanalyst Donald W. Winnicott took religious beliefs away from being considered "pathological" and linked them with a "normal" development of early childhood.

Often we observe infants' and small children's intense preoccupation with their special teddy bears. Winnicott named such a teddy bear a "transitional object." The transitional object becomes the first item that represents "not me" in the child's mind. Although this first "not-me" image corresponds to a thing that actually exists in the world, the transitional object is not entirely "not me," because it is also a substitute for the child's mother, whom the child's mind does not yet fully understand is a separate individual in her own right and whom the toddler perceives to be under his or her absolute control—an illusion, of course (Greenacre 1970). Through a special teddy bear (or a melody that is utilized as a transitional phenomenon) the child begins to know the surrounding world. It is not part of the child, so it signifies the reality "out there" that the child slowly discovers and "creates." What is "created" at first does not respond to reality as perceived by an adult through logical thinking. The child's "reality," while playing with a transitional object or preoccupied with a transitional phenomenon, is a combination of reality and illusion. Winnicott wrote: "Transitional objects and transitional phenomena belong to the realm of illusion which is at the basis of initiation of experience. . . . This intermediate area of experience, unchallenged in respect of its belonging to inner or external (shared) reality, constitutes the greater part of the infant's experience, and throughout life is retained in the intense experiencing that belongs to the arts and to religion and to imaginative living, and to creative scientific work" (Winnicott 1963, p. 242).

Recent psychodynamic interest in religion focuses on how humans use it for hurting Others (Thomson with Aukofer 2011; Volkan 2013). The English term "fundamentalism" as it relates to religion was coined in the United States in the late 1920s. "The Fundamentals" was a series of pamphlets sponsored by California oil tycoons Lyman and Milton Stewart, which outlined five elements of Christian orthodoxy that defined fundamentalism at that time: infallibility of the Bible, the virgin birth, Christ's atonement and resurrection, authenticity of miracles, and dispensationalism (Balmer 1989). The dramatic social changes of the era made the United States ripe for the acceptance of religious fundamentalism, as large numbers of people looked for ways to support their large-group identity. Urban centers supplanted rural ones in the economic power structure, as the country's agricultural economy became less important than the new industrial one. Large numbers of new immigrants, too, changed the social face of the nation.

The size of the membership and the scope of the influence of a cult, *tariqat* or sect are somewhat limited and not globalized. We can find many examples of *restricted* extreme religious movements or cults that have made headlines: Jim Jones' Temple in Jonestown, David Koresh's Branch Davidians in Waco, Shoko Asahara's Japanese Aum Shinrikyo, Joseph DiMambro's Order of Solar Temple, Gush Emunim in Israel and even, in their initial stages, Hamas in Lebanon and Mullah Omar's Taliban in Afghanistan. These all can be considered restricted religious organizations (Mayer 1998; Weber 1999; Wessinger 1999; Moses-Hrushovski 2000; and Volkan 2004). Between February 28 and April 19, 1993, a restricted fundamentalist religious group, Branch Davidians, located in Waco, Texas was surrounded by United States Federal and Texas state law enforcement and United States military. On April 19, 1993 the siege ended with the death of seventy-four men, women and children. In 1995 Vamık Volkan was invited to chair a Select Advisory Commission to the FBI's Critical Incident Response Group charged with examining how insights from behavioral sciences and other branches of societal studies could enhance the agency's ability to respond to crises such as the one at Waco. His chairing the FBI Committee's work lasted for a couple of months. While listening to testimonies given by some individuals from the FBI and discussing the findings with the other members of the committee, Volkan was able to observe the negativity toward the Branch Davidians and David Koresh that was harbored by the authorities throughout the siege at Waco and realized that this negativity had inadvertently fed the Branch Davidians' expectations of an imminent millennial catastrophe. These close-up observations regarding the Waco tragedy provided an opportunity for Volkan to begin to discover and examine some common characteristics of restricted extreme fundamentalist organizations. He was also able at a later date to spend time with a peaceful fundamentalist religious organization, the Old Believers Community in the Lake Peipsi region of Estonia (Volkan 2004). Time spent learning about these restricted religious fundamentalist organizations provided him with a necessary foundation upon which he could stand to take a closer look at more generalized or globalized violent fundamentalist religious movements like al-Qaeda, al-Shabaab and now Boko Haram and ISIS (Volkan 2013).

The monotheistic religions are almost by definition more tempted than the polytheistic or animistic ones to declare their own religion—or its interpretation—the only correct one. A cult, *tariqat* or sect can be defined as a group that is controlled by a charismatic leader who carries an exclusive message from God, who fosters the idea that there is only one correct belief and one correct practice and who demands unquestioning obedience and loyalty (Cushman 1984). The main issues are related to what parts of the religion are cherry-picked and how they are interpreted (McCants 2015). Generalized or even globalized extreme and violent fundamentalist religious movements, as we will show in the next chapter, share most of the same basic elements that exist in restricted movements and, in most cases, start in similar ways. When an extreme and violent religious fundamentalist movement becomes generalized or globalized, it may become contaminated with ethnic, nationalistic, economic, ideological and political issues. When the "bystanders" within the same large group become emotionally involved in the activities of extreme and violent religious fundamentalism, we begin to face a very complicated large-group process that can be best illuminated by the application of psychoanalytic large-group psychology.

Vamık Volkan and Sağman Kayatekin (2006; also see: Volkan 2013) listed the following characteristics of cults or other restricted extreme religious fundamentalist movements.

1. *A divine text*: Whether it is written as scripture or handed down verbally, every restricted extreme religious fundamental movement believes unconditionally in its own " divine text." This may be a particular version of the Bible or interpretation of the Quran, and it is seen as absolute truth and nonnegotiable. For Gush Emunim, for example, relinquishing any land deemed "Land of Israel" would violate God's command and be unthinkable.

2. *An absolute leader who is the interpreter of the divine text*: The leader of a restricted extreme religious fundamentalist movement is the only interpreter of the group's divine text. There is no room for any other interpretations. The leader is usually male—women leaders of these groups are rare—and occasionally, if the leader lacks charisma, he may

choose a "front man." In the case of the Order of the Solar Temple, for example, physician Luc Jouret appeared to be its leader, but the founder was really Joseph DiMambro, who controlled things behind the scenes as they prepared for the return of Jesus Christ in solar glory.

3. *Total loyalty*: A sense of belonging is a key feature for members in a cult, *tariqat* or sect. In well-run extreme restricted religious organizations, everything the followers do and the thoughts they have are organized and institutionalized. Total loyalty to the leader and complete belief in the divine texts remove any potential for anxiety or psychological conflict that might arise. Economic dependence and tangible incentives ensure that members remain in the group. In fact, it becomes very difficult, if not impossible, for a person to leave the group once he or she has joined. The putative divine rule infiltrates every aspect of a member's existence and personal relationships, fundamentally changing them.

4. *Members feel omnipotent, yet victimized*: Restricted extreme fundamentalist religious groups are pessimistic (Sivan 1985) because their members believe that their specific religious "fundamentals" are perpetually under attack by many others, such as non- or even lukewarm believers, Darwinists, Freudians, scientists and rival religious fundamentalist groups who believe that other texts are truly divine.

5. *Extreme masochistic and/or sadistic acts*: Any threat to the survival of the restricted extreme religious fundamentalist group's identity, or a threat to its leader's divine authority, will trigger a preoccupation with the group's protection. Because their pessimism is contaminated with omnipotence, the members may feel entitled to destroy Others who are perceived as threatening the group's survival. For example, in 1980, in Kano, Nigeria, sect leader Alhaji Mohammadu (Maitatsine) Marva, who had proclaimed a new era of antimaterialist reformed Islam, led his followers to the central mosque in Kano, where "nonbelievers" or "lukewarm believers" of his ideas were gathered. This event led to the killing of an estimated 8,000 people. A group can also express its omnipotence by a grand masochistic gesture such as a massive suicide.

Those who kill themselves believe that through death they will merge with the divine leader and/or God, the omnipotent object, and thus crystallize their omnipotence and continue their existence in Paradise.

6. *Shared new "morality"*: Extremely violent restricted religious fundamentalist groups share an alternative "morality" that elevates their own superiority over others who are not "true believers" and sometimes finds mass killings and even mass suicides as acceptable.

7. *Creation of borders*: In addition to building physical borders such as walls or barricades, even when there are no visible threats, members of a cult, *tariqat* or sect build psychological borders around themselves. These may manifest as clothing of a particular style or color designating their separation from others, such as women's head scarves that might be a certain color or be worn in a particular way. In Turkey one fundamentalist group's scarf serves as a uniform symbolizing a border between women in the group and the Other. Israeli men in the Haredi community seclude themselves in yeshivas to study scriptures in isolation from worldly culture and knowledge.

8. *Changing of family, gender and sexual norms within the "borders"*: As a leader of an extreme and restricted religious fundamentalist movement becomes more divine and omnipotent, he or she may serve the roles of "father," "mother" and "lover" for all the followers. "Family values," structures and systems and traditional child-rearing practices dramatically change, replaced by practices ordained by the leader's divine inspirations and interpretations. Women are usually relegated to providing sex (pleasure) and food (milk) to the leader and other males of the group, although often the leader will "own" all the women and children. David Koresh was typical of extreme religious fundamentalist organization leaders (Volkan 2004) who wish to "change" their early troubled childhoods by creating a new "family" with themselves as the wished-for parent. Inevitably, this fails and the new family follows the pattern of the leader's original one, becoming dysfunctional. Koresh owned all the women at the Waco compound—

the men there were celibate—and he had sex with underage girls.

Having sex with underage girls is a symbolic, pathological act by the leader to revise his original internalized "bad" mother-child relationship, although it is explained by "magical" religious beliefs. David Koresh, for example, was born out of wedlock to a very young mother, and, until the age of five, he believed that his aunt was his mother. He was convinced he could not be Jesus Christ because Jesus had no children. Accordingly, he modeled himself after a messiah referred to in Psalm 45, "who married virgins and whose children ruled the earth."

Islamic restricted extreme religious fundamentalist movements also abuse women and children, a practice justified by the "divine book" and its interpreter. When it was first established as a restricted fundamentalist religious group, the Taliban provided a classic example of an Islamic fundamentalist religious movement that was known for its degradation of women in the extreme.

9. *Negative feelings among outsiders*: A restricted extreme fundamentalist religious group feels special, divine, secretive, magical, omnipotent, masochistic or sadistic and erects borders around themselves, so it is understandable that people who live outside their borders have negative feelings toward them. Outsiders may also feel that these groups pose a threat to their own religion or belief system.

11

GLOBALIZED TERRORISM

In 1990 historian Bernard Lewis wrote about "Muslim rage" and noted: "Islamic fundamentalism has given an aim and a form to the otherwise aimless and formless resentment and anger of the Muslim masses at the forces that have devalued their traditional values and loyalties and, in the final analysis, robbed them of their beliefs, their aspirations, their dignity, and to an increasing extent even their livelihood" (Lewis 1990, p. 59). W. Nathaniel Howell, the former U.S. ambassador to Kuwait during its invasion by Saddam Hussein's forces in August 1990 and later Ambassador in Residence at the University of Virginia's Center for the Study of Mind and Human Interaction (CSMHI), referred to what was happening in the Arab world as the "nostalgia movement" for past glories (Howell 1997, p.100). These two scholars specializing in the Middle East noted long before September 11, 2001 that Islamic religious fundamentalism and even its extreme forms would find emotional support within Muslim societies, especially in the Arab world, and that they could easily become globalized. What are the causes of this "Muslim rage" or "nostalgia for past glories"?

Less than a century after the death of the Prophet Muhammed, Arab

Muslim armies had established a huge empire, stretching from India to Spain, and Islamic culture blossomed everywhere. But the unity of Islam was actually broken up very early after the death of the Prophet Muhammed, and there were bitter divisions and regional power struggles almost from the beginning. The most important division had occurred after the fourth Arab Caliph Ali bin Abi Talib (656–661) was killed. A group of Muslims known as Shia rejected the legitimacy of the first three Caliphs in the line of Muhammed. They accepted Muhammed as the prophet and the Quran as divine revelation, but proposed their own interpretation of Quranic law. Today Shia make up 10 to 15 percent of the world's Muslim population, including most of Iran's and Bahrain's Muslims. The majority of the Muslims in Iraq are also Shia. The attack by Sunni Muslims on Al-Askari shrine (one of the holiest Shia sites) in February 2006 and the violent backlash of Shia toward Sunnis in Iraq was a testimony to this old, bloody division within Islam.

There were two major Arab Caliphate dynasties, the Umayyads (661–750) and the Abbasids (750–1258). Between 1261 and 1517 the power belonged to the professional soldiers, the so-called Mamluk sultans of Cairo. The Arab Caliphates came to an end in 1517 when the Turks took over Syria and Egypt during the reign of Ottoman Sultan Selim I (1512–1520), who assumed the title of Caliph and "inherited the role of the defender of the holiest places in Islam, the cities of Mecca and Medina, which were the cradle of Islam" (Itzkowitz 1972, p. 33). The Ottoman Sultans, in their new role as Caliphs (1517–1924), may have been the defenders of the holiest places in Islam, but in truth, none of them ever paid them a visit. Although Islam was a dominant element of Ottoman identity, conquered people from Europe to the Middle East and North Africa were allowed to keep their religions under certain conditions. Muslims certainly had more rights than Christians did in the Ottoman Empire, and there was widespread fear of the Ottomans throughout Europe. Nevertheless, until the decline of the Ottoman Empire in the nineteenth century, the dominant relationship between Christians and Muslims was the relationship between Europe and the Ottoman Empire, as it had been for centuries (Kayatekin 2008). On the other hand, Arabs, who were the first Muslims, now had to live under and submit to the

Ottoman Empire, the Islamic newcomers. Ottoman identity did not adopt an ideology calling for all Muslims to gather under one political umbrella, and the possibility was not even mentioned by either Western or Islamic historians until the nineteenth century (İnalcık 1987; Ortaylı 2003).

Two developments further defined the Western world's perception of the Ottoman Empire and, by extension, of Islam. The first was Europe's preoccupation with "Pan" movements such as Pan-Germanism and Pan-Slavism, which reflected ambition on the part of Germanic or Slavic peoples to create massive entities under the umbrella of their particular ethnicities. Notably, the Russian Empire declared herself the champion of Pan-Slavism and the protector of the Balkan Christians, and used that justification as the *casus belli* in 1877 when declaring war against the Ottoman Empire (the Turco-Russian War of 1877–1878) (Suistola and Tiilikainen 2014). The European elite, seeing the East through the lens of the West, quickly imagined "Pan-Islamism" as originating in Ottoman lands. The second development was the Western powers' interest in Ottoman lands, as the Ottoman Empire was perceived as the "Sick Man of Europe."

These developments and other related events, an in-depth study of which is beyond the scope of this chapter, magnified the idea of an Islamic power even though in the nineteenth century the Ottoman Empire paradoxically was as powerless before as it was after the "Pan" movements. The Western powers, however, thought it best to make the "Sick Man" completely helpless in order to ensure that the danger of a "Pan-Islamic" movement could be contained or removed. There was much competition between European nations at that time as well. Before the First World War (1914–1918) began, Germans bought a number of Ottoman newspapers for propaganda purposes and sent representatives throughout the Ottoman lands. They succeeded in influencing the Ottoman elite and the public in general on the idea that England and France were leading an anti-Islamic movement, while Germany was pro-Islam. The propaganda reached the height of absurdity when it spread rumors that Kaiser Wilhelm II had converted to Islam and made a pilgrimage to Mecca.

Germany utilized a strategy to destabilize regions dominated by British and French influence. The Ottoman elite, by and large, identified with this German propaganda (Kayatekin 2008). The Ottoman Empire entered World War I on the side of Germany, a decision that has generally been viewed as stemming from a German conspiracy supported by Enver Pasha, an organizer   of the Young Turk Revolution of 1908 and a dominant member of the de facto ruling Ottoman "Triumvirate." On the eve of World War I there was a general atmosphere in the Empire to seek revenge after the Balkan Wars. In this, the Ottoman Empire was similar to other European states that presumed war would solve its problems.

Meanwhile, British propaganda was busy spreading a negative image of Ottomans and fear among the British public with the suggestion of a possible united Islamic world under the Ottoman Sultan/Caliph ("a Pan-Islamic Movement") that would destroy the British Empire with the help of Germany. Using this feared and imagined movement to divide and conquer, the British government put out the suggestion that it would prefer to support an Arab Caliph, perhaps someone from among the rulers of Mecca (Kayatekin 2008).

When the Ottoman Empire ended, the Ottoman Sultan's double role as religious leader and political defender of the Islamic world ended as well. The secular Turkish Republic rose from its ashes in 1923 and, under the leadership of Mustafa Kemal (later known as Kemal Atatürk), the Caliphate—in a sense Sunni Islam's "papacy"—was abolished. The centuries-long established leadership of Islam disappeared overnight. One wonders if the present sectarian violence inside of Islam can be partially blamed on Islam's missing central authority. While the Turks tried to establish a new large-group identity—their so-called Westernization struggles—Arabs and many other Muslims remained vulnerable to manipulation by Western powers. For example, even before the Caliphate was abolished, the British continually raised and dashed hopes for establishing a caliphate outside of Turkey, deliberately creating divisions among Indian and Arab Muslims by indicating they would support the establishment of a caliphate in either India or in the Arab world.

The British government's disastrous handling of the Middle East after the collapse of the Ottoman Empire and its humiliation of the Arabs and other Muslims has been analyzed by political scientist Elie Kedourie (1970). According to Kedourie, the highly influential "Chatham House version" of Middle East history, as put forth by British historian Arnold J. Toynbee and his followers, was untrustworthy, was demeaning to the Arabs and contributed to the many failures of the British—and even of the United States—in the Middle East. As a result, chosen traumas and chosen glories of the Arab world have been kept alive, and new ones have taken hold. Even before World War I, believing that the Ottomans would be defeated, the 1916 Sykes-Picot agreement was secretly signed, dividing up the Ottoman territories, including the Ottoman Arab provinces, between the British, the French and the Russians. Events one after another have led to outrage in the Arab world: colonization, as indicated in the 1916 agreement, Western imperialism, the creation of the State of Israel, "green belt" activities (as described earlier) and military invasions. For many in the Arab world, these policies were all experienced as unbearably shameful.

Replacing dysfunctional authoritarian systems with an idealized paternal image of complete authority is a common occurrence in humiliated or regressed societies. The people affected then look for Gods, the Caliphate, or another religious authority. After major societal traumas or struggles for independence, these societies are seldom lucky enough to find leaders such as Kemal Atatürk or Nelson Mandela who will institute progressive programs to increase the society's self-esteem without violently being preoccupied with the Other, and are willing to consider new peaceful means to go forward (Volkan 2004). As we described earlier in this book, under such circumstances often a leader and his or her followers go backward (a regressive move) to re-find realistic or fantasized past glories or even grasp chosen traumas as symbols of their large-group identity. Regressive moves also include grabbing on to religiously tinted images.

Multiple events in recent decades could qualify as starting points if we were to mark the attempt to reverse this humiliation and rejuvenate the glory of Islam, both in Arab and non-Arab countries. The establishment of Dar al Tabligh al-Islami (Institute for the Propagation of Islam) in Iran (MacEoin 1983) is certainly one of them due to the important part it played in creating an atmosphere in Iran that supported the rise of Ayatollah Khomeini and his apocalyptic, millennialist vision for a "perfect" theocracy (Landes 2001). In the late 1980s, however, the Iranian Revolution experienced a loss of prestige in the Muslim world, especially among Sunnis, and Islamist radicals looked elsewhere for inspiration. This was due to economic mismanagement, widespread torture and executions, human rights violations, the Iran-Iraq War and the country's leadership.

"Muslim rage" and "nostalgia for past glories" in the Sunni Arab world, in the end, became the psychological foundation for the globalization of both al-Qaeda and later ISIS. Al-Qaeda searched for the establishment of the Caliphate, and ISIS established it and through propaganda has been trying to make it appear legitimate. This appeal by both Osama bin Laden and Abu Bakr al-Baghdadi to a return to a glorified past, whether realistic or imagined, has found fertile ground.

An analyst has to be careful in writing a psychobiography of a political leader who had not spent time on the psychoanalyst's couch. What a psychoanalyst learns about a patient's life events, internal world and the interaction between the two can serve as a model for finding a continuity of themes in the behavior patterns of a psychobiographical subject's life. Granted, the sophistication of a psychobiographer's final product depends upon the amount of available data, but psychobiography can be a valuable source for understanding the inner world of unique figures in history and how and why they came to influence our world. When Volkan (2004) studied the life stories of David Koresh and Osama bin Laden, he illustrated how in both cases these leaders' traumatic backgrounds played roles in their creating "families," fundamentalist organizations—one restricted and one generalized—in the hope of finding solutions for their personal needs. Nancy Kobrin (2003) and Peter Olsson (2005) also explored known aspects of bin Laden's troubled childhood. We do not have enough information about Abu Bakr al-Baghdadi even to make a preliminary study of his internal world, but here we will provide brief details from these psychobiographical studies that illustrate how bin Laden's internal revengeful psychological motivations may have been reflected in his actions in the external world.

Prophet Muhammed was an orphan who became a spiritual leader and later took up the sword in defense of Islam. Bin Laden too became in essence an "orphan" when he was only one year old and his mother was "exiled" from his father's harem, leaving him in the care of "stepmothers." This was certainly a factor in why he developed a revengeful character. In order to reach up in his developmental ladder, he most likely searched for a father figure since his own father, with so many children from different wives, would not have had much time for him. When Osama was ten, his father died in a plane crash. Then his older brother Salem, who could have been a father or big brother figure for Osama, died tragically and suddenly as well, in a helicopter accident. There are some indications that bin Laden identified with the orphan Muhammed who later became a warrior, so when the time was right, bin Laden stepped forward as a supreme leader with a clear picture of what he wanted to do for Islam and what Islam permits its followers to do. Although they were already in use at the time he took over leadership, this included suicide bombings.

Financial resources made it possible for bin Laden to effectively use propaganda and manipulation. According to bin Laden, "the Islamic world [fell] under the banner of the Cross" (reported by *Africa News Source*, November 5, 2001). Most likely he was also referring to the abolishment of the Caliphate by the Turks. While bin Laden might personally have been concerned about the loss of a father figure (the Caliph) and desired to create a new one with a global and millennial vision, one rarely finds an open reference to the removal of the Caliphate by the Turkish Republic among Muslims on the street in the Arab world and in other Muslim-populated locations. What is more open is the complaint about mistreatment and humiliation by the West within Muslim societies and a corresponding "omnipotence" in anticipating a divine glory based on successful revenge.

One can easily observe nostalgia for past glories of Islam among citizens of Muslim countries. Even in Turkey voices against Atatürk's revolution have been heard for over a decade, as the ruling party has been a religious one. In chapter 9 we described how this party has made open efforts to change the country's large-group identity and turn it into one immersed in religion. The present president of the Turkish Republic, Recep Tayyip Erdoğan, and some authorities in the present government and the ruling political party often speak about Islam and the glorious past of the Ottoman Empire and its military might. Even fantasized and ridiculous-sounding wishes for the return of the Sultanate and the Caliphate to Turkey is heard in the public arena. This, in turn, has caused a severe fragmentation among its citizens, making it very difficult, psychologically speaking, to find a peaceful solution for ethnic issues in Turkey, inflamed by the actions of the PKK, including terrorism, and the Turkish government's response to it.

On the surface, the characteristics of a globalized extreme religious movement seem different than those of restricted extreme religious groups. For example, today's radical Islamist organizations such as al-Qaeda and ISIS resemble giant global commercial corporations, with secret funds and perhaps secret representatives in various countries and with a shared ideology contaminated with religious beliefs. Al-Qaeda and ISIS strive to become world powers by using any means, from engaging in effective political and religious propaganda, to making financial deals. But they also perform horrendous acts of violence. Radical Islam, in general, complains about the Western giant and the merciless commercial/cultural/religious organizations that have infiltrated the Muslim world through "globalization," and which are humiliating Muslims. Nevertheless, al-Qaeda and ISIS have become, in a sense, a more drastic and deadly mirror image of the Western globalization movement. They wish and attempt to globalize their version of extreme fundamentalist Islam. Nevertheless, the characteristics that we can see clearly in restricted extreme fundamentalist religious movements are present within globalized extreme Islamist fundamentalist religious movements as well. A "divine" ideology is present and its "interpreters" exist. These interpreters have declared the United States and the West in general the enemy and "received permission" from Quranic passages such as Surah 8, verse 17 to strike at the "enemy." Followers blindly follow the leader(s) and the ideology. They feel victimized but now omnipotent, and experience an altered "morality." Even when we may not know where they are and where they are hiding, they have built psychological "borders" around themselves in order to maintain their large-group identity. The "us and them" or "We and Others" emphasis illustrates the psychological border. The "divine" ideology replaces family values and many old traditional and religious beliefs, including beliefs about suicide and homicide. Today's extreme fundamentalist Islamist terrorists create strong negative feelings in "outsiders," even in faraway places. But, they also induce hidden or open support among some in foreign lands who may themselves become potential recruits for these terrorist organizations. As we know, thousands of such individuals traveled to Syria to join ISIS.

12

SUICIDE BOMBERS

While fighting with an enemy, fighters do their best to stay alive, but even in ordinary warfare there are exceptions to this rule. During the First World War millions and millions of soldiers marched to an almost certain death without major hesitation, such as during the Battle of Verdun in 1916 when the French and German casualties were about 315,000 and 280,000, respectively. Toward the end of the Second World War Japan systematically began using suicide pilots, more popularly known as kamikaze ("divine wind") pilots. In 2011, John Orbell and Tomonori Morikawa (2011) published a study on the kamikaze pilots based on the letters, wills and poems of 661 of them. The study shows that "honorable" or "beautiful death" was the motivation for suicide for 71.0 percent of the pilots, and the belief that their contribution to the war effort was critical was the motivation for 26.9 percent of these pilots. Meanwhile, 36 percent of the pilots believed that they were going to commit suicide for their country, whereas only 2.9 percent would die for their parents. Religious motivation was nonexistent for the Japanese kamikaze pilots. Kamikaze attacks represented one prominent trait in human behavior: altruism—a selfless devotion to the welfare of others, in this case for Japan, in which an individual risked his personal welfare and even life. What interests us here with regard to our present study is the clear difference between these earlier suicide pilots and present suicide bombers linked to extreme Islamist religious fundamentalist beliefs. Earlier suicides happened within the framework of conventional warfare while targeting the enemy's military. Today, suicide bombers target innocent civilians.

From the end of World War II until the Islamic Revolution in Iran in 1979, no suicide attacks occurred anywhere in the world. When Iran was in a desperate position at the early stages of the war between Iran and Iraq, which lasted from 1980 to 1988, Supreme Leader Ayatollah Ruhollah Khomeini introduced a new weapon to the battlefield, child suicide bombers, and initiated a culture of martyrdom. The first martyr was thirteen-year-old Muhammed Hossein Fahmideh, who destroyed a tank in a suicide attack. After him, thousands of children were recruited as suicide bombers (Caschetta 2015). Later, Hezbollah, a Shia Islamist militant group based in Lebanon, used this new "weapon." Hezbollah's first suicide bombing attack took place on November 1982 when a vehicle full of explosives hit the Israeli military headquarters in Tyre, South Lebanon and killed ninety people. After this event many terrorist organizations began using the same method. The statistics show a horrible trend in suicide bombings: in the 1980s there were forty-two attacks with 805 fatalities and in the 1990s 115 attacks with 1,331 fatalities. Between 2000 and 2004 there were 210 attacks with 4,839 fatalities (Berman 2009). This growth trend has continued, especially with the rise of ISIS. When ISIS took over the city of Ramadi in 2015, the spearhead of the assault was a group of thirty suicide bombers driving vehicles loaded with several tons of bombs. While most suicide attacks are carried out by men, a growing number are carried out by women, with groups such as Boko Haram, al-Shabaab, the Taliban, and ISIS all relying on female suicide bombers as a tactic. The Tamil Tigers first introduced women as suicide bombers in 1987, and in early 2002, Yasser Arafat gave his famous "army of roses" speech, in which he called on women to martyr themselves.

Just as the nature, focus, and scope of terrorist organizations have changed dramatically over the past two decades, so too has the recruitment and training of suicide bombers. In the late 2000s Vamık Volkan spent four months in Israel as an Inaugural Yitzhak Rabin Fellow at the Rabin Center for Israeli Studies in Tel Aviv. This gave him an opportunity to study the creation of Middle Eastern Muslim suicide bombers, a project that he had started some years earlier (Volkan 1997). He learned that in the 1990s and 2000s there was little difficulty in finding young Palestinian men, and even women, interested in becoming suicide bombers. The actual and anticipated events that continually humiliated Palestinian young people also interfered with their adaptive identifications with their parents, since the parents were also being constantly humiliated. The mental representations of external events, along with helplessness and feelings of being treated as less than human, create "cracks" in an individual's identity. Those who selected the "bomber candidates," Volkan found, had developed a good sense of whose identity gaps were most suitable to fill with elements of large-group identity. These candidates would be more easily guided by large-group psychology to carry out murderous and suicidal acts. Muslim suicide bombers found plenty of approval, conscious and unconscious, from other members of this traumatized society as well.

At that time, suicide bombers were recruited and trained in specific ways. "Teachers" would seek out young people whose personal identities were already damaged and who were looking for an outer "element" to internalize so they could stabilize their internal world. The method of teaching involved forcing the religious or ethnic large-group identity into the "cracks" of the person's disturbed or subjugated identity.

Eli Berman (2009) has informed about the work of Ariel Merari, an Israeli psychologist who interviewed failed Palestinian suicide bombers and the families of successful ones. The findings illustrated that these individuals were not mentally ill. They did not use drugs or alcohol and were not depressed. In one notable case during the Second Intifada, al-Fatah tried to use a mentally impaired youngster as a suicide bomber. The youngster was captured, and al-Fatah was heavily criticized by the Palestinians for such an attempt.

Volkan learned that, typically, the "education" of the young Palestinian candidates for suicide attacks was carried out in small groups. These young people experienced conflict with the Israelis as a constantly bleeding wound. Good candidates could be educated quickly, but usually some time was required as the small groups read the Quran together and chanted scripture. One example from the Quran justifies what Bernard Lewis has called "Muslim rage" (Lewis 1990, pp. 47–60) toward the West, especially Israel: "Allah does not forbid you to deal justly and kindly with those who fought not against you on account of religion nor drove you out of your homes. Verily, Allah loves those who deal with equity. ... It is only as regards to those who fought against you on account of religion, and have driven you out of your homes, and helped to drive you out, that Allah forbids you to befriend them ..." (Surah 60, Verses 8 and 9).

Recruits were asked to chant repeatedly mystical-sounding but actually nonsensical phrases such as, "I will be patient until patience is worn out from patience." The repetition of such phrases along with readings from the Quran created a kind of alternate reality, compounded by isolation from families and anything "worldly" that could stimulate sexuality, such as media or music. Although many of these young people's parents must have suspected what their children were doing, suicide bomber candidates were forbidden to inform them of their mission. Having secrets from their parents gave them an added sense of power—a false sense of individuation inflamed by large-group identity, symbolized by cutting off everyday familiar dependency. Once a person became a suicide bomber candidate, routine rules and regulations of individual psychology did not fully apply to patterns of thought and action. The person became an agent of the large-group identity and would attempt to repair it for him- or herself and for other members of the large group. Killing one's self (and one's personal identity) and "Others" (enemies) was less important than the act of bombing (terrorism) that would bring self-esteem and attention to the large-group identity and keep the large-group identity "alive."

The future suicide bombers did not see their mission as suicide. Instead, emphasis was on their performing an act of martyrdom (Hafez 2006). Indeed, in Islam, suicide bombings constitute a doctrinal problem: suicide is *haram*, a forbidden act. The *haram* rule has thus been circumvented by renaming suicide bombing "tactical martyrdom" and "altruistic murder." Ayman al-Zawahiri, the leader of al-Qaeda since the death of Osama bin Laden, formulates the difference thusly: ending one's life out of depression is suicide and ending it to serve Islam is martyrdom (Caschetta 2015).

Playing the immortality card, the "teachers" used the Prophet

Muhammad's instructions to his followers during the Battle of Badr (624 C.E.), which some consider one of the earliest examples of war propaganda, as part of their training. Mohammad assured his followers that if they should die in battle, they would continue to live in Paradise. Suicide bomber recruits were told that once they became martyrs all their sexual and dependency needs would be fulfilled by *houris*, beautiful maidens who live in Paradise. Killing themselves was like a rite of passage into adulthood for the male recruits, with sex and women as their promised reward. Volkan learned that the death of a male suicide bomber was celebrated as a "wedding ceremony," a celebration at which friends and family gathered to celebrate their belief that the dead terrorist was in the loving hands of angels in heaven. Collectable cards, like baseball cards in the United States, were prepared and distributed, showing the picture of the now dead suicide bomber. Volkan also was told that "wedding ceremonies" and printing collectible cards also induced bad feelings among the Palestinian communities, and these practices were stopped.

With September 11, 2001, the world noted what appeared to be a new profile for radical Islamist suicide terrorists. Previously, most had been young Palestinians who had been humiliated personally or were relatives or friends of those who had been. These new terrorists were mostly from Egypt and Saudi Arabia; they were also older. By all appearances, these were indeed a new breed of terrorist. However, closer scrutiny reveals that the psychological mechanisms that created an earlier generation of radical Islamist suicide terrorists applied to this new group of terrorists as well.

In chapter 2 we described a metaphoric tent covering a large group with its canvas representing this large group's identity. The more this canvas shakes and is perceived to be unstable—not only due to the Other's humiliating attacks but also due to local circumstances—the more individuals are attracted, even if they are rich and educated, to wearing the tent's canvas as their primary garment and trying to stabilize its shaking. Islam, like Christianity, pays great attention to death and life hereafter, but it is the rise of fundamentalist Islam that has helped to create an especially favorable atmosphere for killing oneself—that is, to be a martyr for a large group and to become "immortal" in the collective memory of the large group. Suicide bombers act under the influence of psychology.

Speckhard and Yayla (2015), who interviewed ISIS defectors, note that ISIS prepares recruits to commit extremely violent acts and to be ready to die for a cause bigger than themselves. Parts of holy scripture that support the use of violence to further the religion are strongly emphasized during the training of recruits, including the very young. As UN report S/2016/92 claims, ISIS is "systematically indoctrinating and grooming children as young as five years old to be future militants" (p. 4).

Speckhard and Yayla also report on the future suicide bombers' "graduation ceremonies." According to the information they provide, such ceremonies require a graduate to execute an "enemy" prisoner housed for this purpose near the training camp. According to other accounts, some suicide bombers joined the terrorist organization only a few weeks before they were called upon to attack (Berman 2009). This suggests that they may have been emotionally prepared to be suicide bombers before even joining the group and thus only a very short period of "training" for such recruits.

The November 2015 Paris and March 2016 Brussels attacks illustrate another dimension of recent terrorist attacks in the West. Instead of acting as lone wolves, the attackers formed small grassroots cells of radical Islamists who also had Western citizenship. The core of such cells is often formed by siblings, such as in the case of the January 2015 Boston Marathon bombing, or by those related in some other way. For example, in September 2015, a married couple carried out attacks in San Bernardino, California.

From a tactical perspective, suicide bombers are, unfortunately, very efficient "weapons" for terrorism. As we described earlier, as weapons capable of doing considerable damage go, they are relatively low cost. Also, if it is successful, no informant will be left behind. Further, the explosives can be delivered in various ways to varying degrees, whether in bomb belts, cars or airplanes. Even if a plan must be altered, the capacity or causing significant injury and death remains. Other forms of "suicide" attack that require even less expense or even training are being employed. For example, on July 14, 2016, Mohamed Lahouaiej-Bouhlel killed eighty-six people in Nice by driving a cargo truck into a Bastille Day crowd, before being shot by police. This method of attack was suggested in the *Inspire* magazine of al-Qaeda as early as 2011. In some cases, the attacker even manages to escape from the scene, as in the cases of Anis Amri, who killed twelve people in Berlin when he smashed a stolen truck into a Christmas market on December 19, 2016, and Abdulkadir Masharipov, the gunman who killed thirty-nine at the Reina nightclub in Istanbul on January 1, 2017.

But it is not only the destructiveness that counts. A terrorizing factor is achieved: everyone is made to feel like a potential target while they are at a coffee shop, metro station, airport or wedding ceremony. Tourism usually drops dramatically in countries where suicide attacks regularly take place. It is observed that locals return to their daily routines in weeks, rather than months, and start shopping and using the metro stations where the attack happened. For tourists to return to their favorite cities, it might take a bit longer. Collective fear of jihadist suicide bombers has become inflamed in Europe due to recent terrorist attacks, such as those in France and Belgium. When suicide bombings occur in other parts of the world, whether in Africa or the Middle East, American media coverage is very limited. For example, in May 2016, there were terrorist attacks in 44 Iraqi cities—39 of them in Baghdad. These tragedies were hardly mentioned in American and Western media. But when suicide bombings occur in Europe, the American coverage of such an event goes on for many days.

We conclude this chapter with Jouni Suistola's graphic illustrating his *Funnel Model*. The model is connected with the observations we presented earlier: a stable society with political rights rarely gives birth to terrorism; an unstable society in conflict paves the road to terrorism, with the creation of suicide bombers at its end. As shown in the graphic, the path through the funnel itself becomes narrower and narrower, dramatically decreasing the chances that the potential bomber will reverse his or her process (see figure 4).

FIGURE 4. ROAD TO BECOMING A TERRORIST AND SUICIDE BOMBER

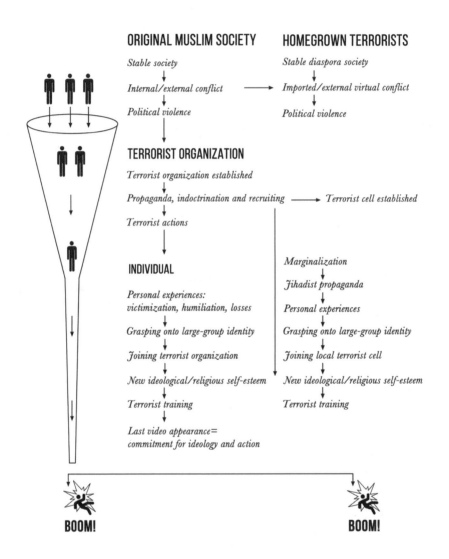

13

LESSONS IN DEALING WITH TERRORISM

Since September 11, 2001, the United States and countries across the globe have been heavily involved in counterterrorism operations. Yet, during the same time period, terrorism has dramatically increased. Some of this is due to the inflaming of the causes of terrorism, as discussed in the previous chapters, but might something be wrong with accepted counterterrorism practices and might efforts to deal with violence and terror be inadequate? Furthermore, are there even any good options for countering present-day terrorism?

The Middle East conflict, especially the interaction between Palestinians and Israelis, has become, in a sense, a large-scale "laboratory" for developing and implementing methods not only for terrorism, but also for counterterrorism. In this chapter, from a historical perspective, we will look at Israel's dealings with terrorism (Byman 2011) and then review aspects of the United States' efforts concerning extreme jihadists. Before focusing on the conflict between Israelis and Palestinians, we should remember that Jews had established their own terrorist organizations in their struggle against the British and Palestinians before May 14, 1948, the day the State of Israel was proclaimed. For example, in 1938, the militant Zionist group Irgun launched a bomb attack at a Haifa marketplace, killing dozens of Arabs, and its attack on the King David Hotel in Jerusalem in 1946 killed ninety-one people.

The Palestine National Liberation Movement (al-Fatah), a political movement, was established in 1959 by members of the Palestinian diaspora, including Yasser Arafat, and in 1967, it joined the Palestine Liberation Organization (PLO), becoming its largest constituent faction. Following the 1970 civil war in Jordan, PLO and al-Fatah fighters ended up in Lebanon after being expelled from Jordan by the Jordanian Army . These Palestinians eventually helped push Lebanon into a civil war (1975–1990). In 1978 Israel launched Operation Litani in South Lebanon, the first of several military operations on that front, and took over control of Lebanon up to the Litani River. When the Israel Defense Forces (IDF) left the area, then also known as "Fatahland," Palestinians returned there. Because this region was not "pacified," Israel launched a bigger military operation in 1982 with the aim of defeating the Palestinians in Lebanon and forcing them to accept Israeli rule over Gaza and West Bank. The IDF marched to Beirut and forced al-Fatah and Yasser Arafat to leave Lebanon. Then the Lebanese Christian Phalangists attacked two Palestinian refugee camps, Sabra and Shatila, at the outskirts of Beirut and massacred about 3,500 people there, including children. Responsibility for the Sabra and Shatila massacres landed at Israel's doorstep because the IDF had the duty of protecting these camps. We can consider the rise of Hezbollah, the Shia Islamist militant group in Lebanon, to be a consequence of this event. From the Israeli perspective the positive outcome was that al-Fatah was expelled from Lebanon to Tunisia, and its threat to Israel was reduced. Meanwhile, the long-term Israeli occupation of South Lebanon was costly. In 1990, Vamık Volkan visited a Palestinian orphanage in Tunis, Tunisia, Beit Atfal al-Sumud (the House of Steadfast Children). There, he observed five children who had been found as babies at Sabra and Shatila after the massacres. They had been given the surname "Arafat" (Volkan 1997). Most of the orphans said they often dreamt of becoming pilots in the future and then flying to and bombing Israel.

Israel would later use a similar military strategy in dealing with the Second Intifada in 2001, when it carried out attacks in the West Bank, and in Gaza in 2008–2009 and 2014. Moreover, Israel launched a military operation against Hezbollah in South Lebanon in June 2006. This time the Israeli military lost around 120 soldiers and, three months after the military operation began, started withdrawing from Lebanon.

The military operations mentioned here illustrate a strategy to drive terrorists out of a certain territory, or at least to establish control there. They were an essential part of the Israeli efforts to prevent terrorism through deterrence. This strategy included inflicting pain on one's enemy. The enemy's suffering must be disproportionate to the strategist's own pain. For example, during the 2008–2009 Gaza war, 1,400 Palestinians were killed. The Israelis, meanwhile, suffered a much smaller number of deaths—13 total.

Targeted killings have constituted another element of deterrence for Israelis; they destroy the operational capabilities of the terrorist organizations by killing their leaders, recruiters, bomb makers and other key individuals. Targeted killings are carried out by using missiles, drones, snipers, special commandos and agents. In some cases such killings have also taken place primarily for revenge. For example, after the Munich Olympic Games attack in 1972, Mossad's campaign Operation Wrath of God led to the assassinations of Black September operatives in several foreign countries. Interestingly enough, it was not Mossad but Yasser Arafat who finished Black September. By 1973, the organization had turned from a valuable asset for the Palestinians' cause to a burden. Al-Fatah found wives for the Black September operatives, offered them homes in Damascus and provided them with allowances. This was a rare and nonviolent way to end a terrorist organization, by literally taming its members.

Israel has developed other means for territorial control and for increasing security, including the construction of a wall along the Green Line and in the West Bank and the ongoing blockade of Gaza, which is further enhanced by Egypt at its border with Gaza. Israel has also exerted territorial control through the establishment and expansion of settlements.

Although the wall helped curb attacks on Israel launched from the West Bank, mortar shells and rockets can easily traverse a wall or blockade and remain a threat. Due to the imprecise nature of shelling and rocket attacks, targets of such attacks, when launched, are largely random. The Israelis have typically countered such attacks, which have lead to civilian deaths, by targeting those responsible for launching the missiles or by destroying the rockets with their so-called Iron Dome antimissile system. Here, we face one of the main structural problems of counterterrorism efforts—grossly disproportionate expenses. One al-Qassam (the simple homemade Palestinian rocket) costs about $50, while one Iron Dome missile costs about $50,000.

After the Second Intifada, in 2003, Israel withdrew from populated Palestinian areas and began to control the West Bank with a system of roadblocks, gates, trenches, earth mounds and manned checkpoints. By 2009, Israel had established more than 600 obstacles to passage inside the West Bank and sixty-three controlled crossing points between the West Bank and Israel. While such disruptions and barriers do nothing to salve the sense of humiliation and grievance felt by Palestinians, this infrastructure of control makes it difficult for terrorist organizations to smuggle weapons or even to have meetings or communicate face to face among themselves. Much of their communication thus takes place through the Internet and mobile phones, which are vulnerable to Israeli eavesdropping.

Maintaining some sense of security in the face of terrorist threats has been a heavy burden for Israel—not only militarily and economically but also ethically and morally, especially as relates to human rights and suffering. In the 1990s, in the wake of the Oslo Accords, Israel not only recognized the Palestinian Authority (PA) but also handed over to them a major role in maintaining security, even arming PA's police force with light weapons. This marked a major change in Israeli security philosophy and the results were mainly positive. Unfortunately, this effort collapsed with the Second Intifada.

In addition, Israel has used collective severe punishments, such as curfews and house demolitions. Needless to say, collective punishments cannot be considered justified from a humane point of view, although they are presented from the angle of counterterrorism and positioned not as punishment, but deterrence. By punishing innocent outsiders who happen to be relatives of terrorists, Israelis hope to compel extended family members and communities to stop terrorist activities by others within their families and communities in order to avoid collective punishment. Efraim Benmelech, Esteban K. Flor and Claude Berrebi (2013) claim that targeting the houses of terrorists decreased the number of terrorist attacks significantly, but curfews and random house demolitions increased the terrorist attacks, at least during the Second Intifada. They wrote: "The results support the view that selective violence is an effective tool to combat terrorist groups and that indiscriminate violence backfires" (p. 1).

Israel has also tried to "clean" the terrorists out. There are several ways to do that: deportations, denial of work or residence permits and arrests. The last method is the most traditional one for this purpose. During the First Intifada in 1989 Israel arrested 13,000 Palestinians. Arrests can be "productive" for two purposes: gathering information through interrogations and turning the militants into Israeli informants. Recently Israel has claimed that they have about 20,000 Palestinian collaborators— the figure may be correct, but it could also be publicized in an attempt to sow mistrust within Palestinian society.

Almost all of the Israeli counterterrorism activities mentioned above are based on the use of violence or intimidation. In the long run, these efforts have either failed or at least presented a "high price" to be paid. There is a totally different path to walk, namely, the one leading to a negotiated agreement to end terrorism. Indeed, Israel has walked that path on several occasions. The most prominent attempt so far was the Oslo Accords, which began as a series of "track-two" or unofficial contacts between Israelis and Palestinians facilitated by the Norwegians. An earlier track-two process spearheaded by the American Psychiatric Association's Committee of Psychiatry and Foreign Affairs brought together influential Israelis and Egyptians for unofficial dialogues between 1980 and 1986. In the third year of these gatherings Palestinian representatives also joined in the process. In fact, the term "tract-two diplomacy" was coined in a *Foreign Policy* article by the first chairperson of the American Psychiatric Association committee, William Davidson, and a U.S. diplomat who was appointed as a member of this committee as a liaison to the U.S. Department of State, Joseph Montville (Davidson and Montville 1981–1982; Montville 1990).

Vamık Volkan's membership in the Committee of Psychiatry and Foreign Affairs started in 1978. Three years after the Committee began to bring influential Israelis and Egyptians together, Volkan assumed its leadership. He has described in detail what happened during these dialogues and their consequences (Volkan 1988, 1997, 2013, 2014c). What is important here is acknowledgment that a human factor, the psychology of a political leader, played the key role in changing the chronic stubbornness of a severe international conflict by opening an opportunity to attempt peaceful solutions instead of looking for resolution through violence. In the preface we described how then president of Egypt Anwar el-Sadat went to Israel in 1977 to address the Knesset. He described a "wall" between Israelis and Egyptians and in fact all Arabs. He said: "This wall constitutes a psychological barrier between us, a barrier of suspicion, a barrier of rejection; a barrier of fear, of deception, a barrier of hallucination without any action, deed or decision…. A barrier of distorted and eroded interpretation of every event and statement. It is this psychological barrier which I described in official statements as constituting 70 percent of the whole problem." The American Psychiatric Association's Committee's project to establish and experiment with an unofficial negotiation process was inspired by Sadat's visit to Israel. When Volkan was an Inaugural Yitzhak Rabin Fellow in Israel in 2000 he learned that until Sadat's actual arrival in Israel, the Israelis did not believe that his visit would take place. Fearing that the airplane flying to Israel might not be carrying Sadat, but armed terrorists instead, Israelis had a military team, hidden from public eye, with guns aimed at the approaching airplane until the Egyptian president actually stepped out.

The Oslo process resulted in the mutual recognition of the opposing parties, the state of Israel and the PLO. Although the Oslo Accords were signed in Washington, DC in 1993 and Taba, Egypt in 1995, from the very beginning two major problems were apparent: even though milestones were laid out in the accords, no means of how to reach them were in place, and it was not clear who would control and guarantee the progress or how. Volkan (2013) has written about an associated psychological difficulty that warrants recognition and attention in such circumstances, the "accordion phenomenon." Imagine someone playing an accordion, squeezing and then expanding it. Realistic discussions between the representatives of opposing large groups cannot take place when the accordion is squeezed too much or is expanded too much. If the enemy groups are "forced" to come too close and "love" one another, this leads to a negative response, because too much closeness is perceived as mixing large-group identities, and this causes anxiety. The Oslo Accords represented a squeezing of the "accordion." Following the signing of the accords, peacemakers did not seriously work on the "accordion" to keep it playing until the extreme squeezing and extreme expanding disappeared. The peace effort eventually collapsed with the Second Intifada.

The United States has been actively involved in the Israel-Palestine peace process for decades, and Americans, whether government officials or civilians, have also been involved with many other Middle East confidence-building efforts, some of them useful and others ineffective. Nothing has worked to establish a stable peace and a stable solution for the so-called Palestinian issue. Continuing problems include fluctuating discussions between a two-state solution and one-state solution, Israel's refusal to talk with Hamas, questions regarding the right of return, the position of Jerusalem, Israeli control of borders, Gaza's incredibly bad economic conditions, severely disaffected Palestinian youth, and so on.

To summarize, the core Israeli counterterrorism efforts have been conventional military air and ground operations to finish off terrorist organizations, to deny them a safe haven or sanctuaries, to curtail their operational freedom or to push them out. Military operations have also been the backbone of Israeli deterrence strategy. Territorial operations have usually aimed at a short- or long-term control of a certain area.

The United States has similarly depended on the large-scale use of military force in its counterterrorism and counterinsurgency operations. Mark Moyar, who is known for his previous writing on the Vietnam War (2009), listed what he calls "The White House's Seven Deadly Errors" in American counterterrorism efforts (2016). He refers to poor judgment and disorganization. For him, the first error was excessive confidence in democratization. In Afghanistan, Iraq and Libya, the United States presumed that military operations would be followed by an overall democratization process leading to a so-called liberal peace. This, however, has not happened.

After Saddam Hussein was removed from power in Iraq in 2003, the United States became involved in years-long counterinsurgency activities in Iraq. Fred Kaplan (2013) claims that the relative success of counterinsurgency in Iraq was not due to American activities, but to the Anbar Awakening, the counterterrorist actions taken by local Sunni sheiks and their militias even prior to the U.S. operation. According to Moyar (2016), another United States mistake was the departure of U.S. forces from Iraq at the end of 2011; it was premature. In Afghanistan the United States defined the closing date of the Afghanistan operation and tried to sort things out with an Iraqi-type surge of troops and by training Afghani military and police. At this moment, it is too early to predict the final outcome in Afghanistan, but the signs are not encouraging.

Moreover, the United States has counted too much on surgical strikes (drones, ambushes and raids) in dealing with terrorists. Strikes by the United States and its allies in Syria and Iraq started in the summer of 2014, and Russian strikes began in the fall of 2015. They have killed as many as 20,000 ISIS fighters and destroyed its economic assets. In addition, by the end of 2016, ISIS had lost as much as 40 percent of its territory in Iraq and Syria. Yet, this has happened mainly on account of ground operations by the Syrian Kurdish militia, *Yekîneyên Parastina Gel* (YPG) (People's Protection Units), and lately much is also due to both Syrian and Iraqi armed forces. As we finalize this book, the Iraqi Armed Forces are just reconquering from ISIS the important city of Fallujah, just 70 kilometers to the west of Baghdad, and the fight over Mosul is still going on. Nevertheless, ISIS, with its approximately 38,000 combatants, presents a serious challenge, not only in Iraq and Syria but also elsewhere, especially in Libya.

Military-based U.S. counterterrorism operations have been expensive in financial terms and lost lives. There are estimations that the overall expenses in Iraq are over two trillion dollars. Furthermore, more than 5,000 American servicemen and -women have been killed in Afghanistan and Iraq. Yet, as noted, these actions have increased terrorist actions and threats.

Drastic historical events kept happening as this book was getting ready to be printed. Among them was Donald Trump's election and subsequent inauguration as president of the United States. He declared he would keep the American people (and, by extension, American identity) safe from unwanted elements, whether immigrants from the South or terrorists from the Middle East. He has repeatedly expressed his determination to build a wall at the U.S.–Mexico border and ban people from entering the United States from various Muslim countries. He also approved the "the mother of all bombs" to be dropped on ISIS in Afghanistan. However, his presidency has faced many complications, with events changing rapidly. We must wait to see whether his administration will introduce new strategies and tactics in dealing with ISIS and other terrorist organizations.

14

NEGOTIATION

A Systemic Approach

Seth Jones and Martin Libicki (2008) from RAND Corporation published a study to illustrate how terrorist groups eventually end. They studied 648 terrorist groups active between 1968 and 2006 and reported on their fate. They concluded that 43 percent of them ended through a political process, 40 percent through policing, 10 percent through the victory of the terrorists and only 7 percent through military success. It appears that this picture has been changing during the last eight years. Jonathan Powell (2014) found that out of those 648 terrorist groups, 244 are still functioning and 136 have transformed themselves into other organizations. As a result, only about 42 percent of the groups have really been closed down. Moreover, the relatively high percentage of successful policing took place when dealing with small leftist groups such as Baader-Meinhof, a group that we cannot really compare with a globalized terrorist organization such as ISIS. Yet, the major point of the Jones and Libicki study is this: military success rarely ends terrorism. This finding is still valid. Nevertheless, sometimes—in fact often—force is necessary to show the terrorists that their violence is not the solution.

To explore counterterrorism further we will now present Jouni

Suistola's systematic approach to this topic based on his observations of terrorist patterns related to al-Fatah (and PFLP), the Tamil Tigers, al-Qaeda, al-Shabaab, Boko Haram and ISIS. Obviously details of terrorist and antiterrorist activities belonging to different organizations vary, but, generally speaking, they follow the same patterns.

In brief, when a terrorist organization is weak, it acts globally and uses a pure terrorist strategy. In turn the main counterterrorism task belongs to intelligence and police forces. When a terrorist organization grows stronger, the responsibility to counter it moves toward military organizations. Finally, when a terrorist organization operates in a geographical region, as ISIS does at the moment, the main counterterrorist activities belong to armed forces.

When a terrorist organization is "weak"—be it at the early stages of its "career" or due to successful counterterrorist operations—it is at the "most terroristic" stage and operates globally. The Armenian Secret Army for Liberation of Armenia (ASALA) and the Japanese Red Army (JRA) are good examples of this pattern: both were relatively small organizations but operated globally. Their actions were based either on lone wolves, local cells or operations launched from the home country, such as the one carried out by the Japanese Red Army at Tel Aviv Airport in May 1972. The same pattern was also exhibited by al-Qaeda during the 1990s and 2000s, when it hit the U.S. embassies in Kenya and Tanzania in August 1998 and the *USS Cole* in Yemen in October 2000. When a terrorist organization becomes stronger, it moves toward a guerilla strategy and aims to control a geographical area. Finally, at the peak of its power a terrorist organization adapts a conventional warfare strategy with a regional territorial control. Although it may launch occasional tactical terrorist operations, they decrease in scale. If a strong terrorist organization loses its power due to counterterrorism activities, it typically starts launching "classical" terrorist attacks globally.

Consider, for a moment, the trajectory of al-Qaeda and the associated trend toward homegrown "cell-based" jihadist terrorism against Western targets, such as the Boston Marathon bombing in April 2013, the *Charlie Hebdo* shooting in January 2015 and the March 2016 attacks in Brussels. First, al-Qaeda lost its "heartland," Afghanistan, and then the central part of its leadership—Osama bin Laden included—was eliminated. Al-Qaeda is experiencing increasing difficulty planning, coordinating and launching operations in the West, and communicating with its Western diaspora cells. Consequently, it has turned to "franchise organizations" with a loose relationship to its "branches." The latest ISIS operations in Belgium, France, Pakistan and Turkey might also indicate the same shift has happened within ISIS. It is clear that ISIS has been pushed from offensive to defensive in its heartland in Iraq and Syria. ISIS is becoming weaker and therefore is "bound" to global terrorist attacks. The cells based on siblings and relatives certainly reflect a psychological factor of attackers sharing common values—family history, even genes, and the same neighborhood such as Molenbeek in Brussels. Another indication of this development is ISIS showing signs of having increasing difficulty recruiting people from Western societies. On the other hand, we have to keep in mind that an estimated 30,000 foreign fighters have joined ISIS's rank and file. So far, the empirical evidence tells us that only very few have committed terrorist attacks after returning to their country of origin, but at the same time their attacks "are more likely to be successful and lethal" (UN Report S/2016/92, p. 13).

Consideration of the trajectory of terrorist organizations can be useful when an opportunity arises to consider utilizing a negotiated solution method to end terrorism. This is a very complicated topic. The usual position of governments is, "We do not negotiate with terrorists" or "We do not talk to jihadists because they are irrational." At the same time, it is very difficult to end terrorism by violent methods alone. Thus, governments and other counterterrorism-related organizations do actually talk with terrorist organizations when and if there is a "window of opportunity." There is another difficulty. Terrorist organizations that highjack religion and cling on their God may also feel omnipotent and divine. Since their God's permission for their activities cannot be questioned it becomes very difficult, if not impossible, for them to negotiate with the Other, especially the Other who is a nonbeliever or who prays to a different God. Gods do not negotiate!

To launch a successful negotiation process, the opposing parties must not only be willing to participate, but also possess a necessary power balance between them. The systematic approach described above illustrates that when the power of a terrorist organization increases, it becomes more conventional and less terroristic. At best, the terrorist organization will leave strategic terrorism behind and reduce in number its tactical terrorist attacks, but if it is weakened again, it will inevitably return to a terrorist strategy (see figure 5). There have been only a few occasions in which violence and talks have successfully "cohabited"; in most cases, violence by either side is a guaranteed way to derail peacemaking. Thus, cessation of violence is usually a precondition for a fruitful negotiation process.

From a systematic approach point of view, a terrorist organization's level of strength also is important for a counterterrorism organization (a government, for example) to start talking with the terrorists. If the terrorists are very strong, they either do not come to the negotiation table, or if they do, they do not negotiate in good faith, but rather play for time or launch a public stunt operation to prove their peace credentials. Furthermore, if they are very strong they do not need to make concessions. On the other hand, if their strength has not reached a "suitable" level, they are not able to make concessions. Simply put, there is no agreement without concessions. The optimal point for negotiations is when the terrorists have been weakened in a "reasonable way," when they have already been forced to swallow some bitter pills and experience a sense of defeat, but when they still have bargaining chips.

In the case of ISIS, a fruitful negotiation process with the organization cannot even be imagined at this time. Indeed, according to UN Security Council Report S/2016/92 (December 2015), a total of thirty-four different groups—from South and Southeast Asia, to Pakistan and Central Asia and to West Africa—have pledged allegiance to ISIS. Military-, intelligence-, and security-based solutions aside, one way to weaken the organization is to find ways to slow or stop its ability to recruit new members, especially through steps to prevent radicalization in the first place. For example, 20 percent of young British Muslims show sympathy toward coreligionists fighting under the banner of ISIS. This represents not only the success of ISIS propaganda, but also demonstrates the poor level of knowledge of Islam among second- and third-generation Muslims in the Western diaspora. Another important factor is at play, as evidenced elsewhere in

FIGURE 5. WINDOW OF OPPPORTUNITY FOR NEGOTIATION

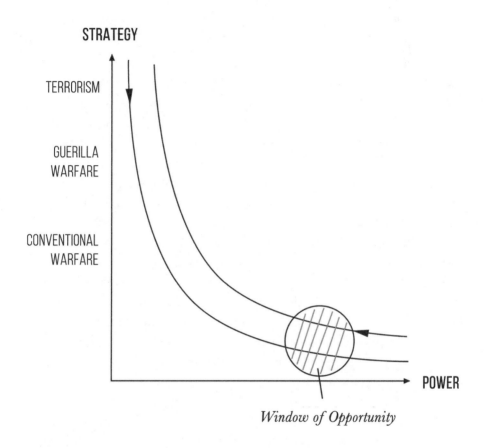

Window of Opportunity

Europe. As the Syrian refugee crisis and terrorist attacks in San Bernardino, Paris and Brussels were taking place, about seventy young people in Finland left the country to join ISIS. One of the main factors for their radicalization was a new atmosphere in Finland—a sense that they no longer belonged. Indeed, the central message in interviews with a few of them who have returned and with their relatives and friends is that their radicalization was connected to their sensing themselves to be aliens in the eyes of Finns, in the country where many of them were born. Each terrorist act committed in the name of Islam only serves to reinforce this sense, creating a vicious cycle.

ISIS propaganda flagrantly pushes ISIS's own version of Islam to justify acts of violent extremism. As the grand mufti of Egypt, Shawki Allam (2015), wrote: "Since terrorist groups have the audacity to interpret from the Quran selectively to suit their own agendas, their deviant ideology must be debunked by intellectual responses. The fight will be stronger with the help of international media and academia in publishing and broadcasting the voices of authentic Muslim scholars who can counter the extremists' false claims and warped interpretation of the Quran" (p. A11). This is an important suggestion, and the idea of teaching about and explaining Islam in the West, instead of objecting to it, can make what is feared less dangerous. But, we see problems in this logical-sounding proposition. Using "Islam" has become incredibly intertwined with politics in many Muslim countries. This makes it very difficult to sort out "the voices of authentic Muslim scholars."

A better and more effective way for making a society in the West less afraid of people with a "foreign" religion or ethnicity or even political ideology is not to get involved in political or educational propaganda against such people in general. Decades ago when communism was the "enemy" in the United States, Americans were taught to dislike and hate the Soviet people in general. Even suspected communists were harassed within the United States under the "ideology" of McCarthyism. Helen Caldicott, a physician who was a member of the 1979 American delegation visiting the Soviet Union as guests of the Soviet Peace Committee, describes negative teaching about the Soviets in the United States. For example, she wrote: "There is a compulsory course taught in the Florida high schools called Americanism vs. Communism (nicknamed AVC by the school children); in Texas, children are taught the evils of communism; other states conduct similar educational campaigns. This sort of childhood conditioning serves to justify the projection of the dark side. Nations behave in this way very much as individuals do" (Caldicott 1986, p. 233).

Considering the poisoned Islamophobic and xenophobic atmosphere in the West, politicians and educators should be active in not allowing this type of "bad" teaching, in this case about Muslims. Considering how sometimes fear and separating and cleansing one group from the Other can create benefits for some politicians, whether in the United States or France, Hungary or the Netherlands, we are aware of difficulties in this method of prevention. There are several interfaith dialogue initiatives in the United States and elsewhere. Some of them are scholarly and serious, such as the Abrahamic Family Reunion project to promote Muslim-Christian-Jewish reconciliation, which is directed by Joseph Montville, while others are contaminated with open or hidden propaganda and motivated by political gain and influence.

Even if religious or any other types of terrorism are contained or finished there is a massive task to complete: what shall be done with people who were terrorists? If the conflict with terrorism ends with a negotiated solution, the agreement can include a reconciliation element. If terrorism is contained or ends in another way, there is another "solution": for example, in January 2016 Saudi Arabia executed forty-seven people convicted on terrorism charges. Among them was a Shia cleric Sheikh Nimr al-Nimr, a critic of Saudi rule (Eikenberry, Weinberg, and Suzano 2016). This "solution," of course, is not acceptable by any modern standard of human rights. Another way is to reintegrate the terrorists into society. This task takes enormous resources even if the number of terrorists is relatively low. For example, in the case of Niger Delta militants, the reintegration program has cost over $1 billion (Ogunlesi 2015). In Saudi Arabia in September 2014 the police arrested eighty-eight suspected al-Qaeda operatives: fifty-nine of them had gone through the reintegration program at the Muhammad bin Nayef Center for Counseling and Care. In the case of the ISIS attack against a Shia mosque in Saudi Arabia, out of seventy-seven arrested suspects, forty-seven had been in the same program (Eikenberry, Weinberg, and Suzano 2016). These programs clearly have not been very successful. In Afghanistan a similar governmental program gained minimal success (Jones 2011).

15

USEFUL SOURCES

History and Psychoanalysis

In this book we explored violent aspects of human nature, including using religion for horrible purposes and globalized terrorism. We approached our subjects mainly from two points of view, historical and psychoanalytic. We also used a systematic approach in explaining some aspects of societal behavior. One of the main starting points of co-operation between some psychoanalysts and historians goes back to William Langer's 1957 Christmas address at the American Historical Association when he was its president. He declared that the next assignment for historians should be paying attention to depth psychology. Vamık Volkan, while he was the director of the University of Virginia's Center for the Study of Mind and Human Interaction from 1987 to 2002, worked closely with historian Norman Itzkowitz from Princeton University and also historian and psychoanalyst Peter Loewenberg from the University of California, Los Angeles in various conflict areas of the world. James William Anderson and Jerome Winer (2003) wrote: "All of history is made by individuals, whether they are leaders, creative thinkers, or members of a grouping of people. As a body of thought that best illuminates the inner world, psychoanalysis has a natural relevance for the study of history. It can help get at the motivations of individuals and groups, it can offer possible explanations for many of history's mysteries, and it can also make sense of relationships between people" (p. 1).

In this book we examined the psychology of individuals and large groups and explained the unconscious but obligatory evolution of individualized and shared prejudice. We inquired about what makes a benign prejudice turn into a malignant one leading to deadly aggression. We illustrated the repetition of similar individual and large-group violent behaviors throughout human history. People from different religions and from different ideologies have been involved in conventional wars, guerrilla struggles and terrorism. We wrote about how humans justify killing the Other, about the links between socio-political conflicts and terrorism, and about political and terrorist propaganda and suicide bombers. We can make a general statement about these historical facts and state that people basically are the same wherever they live. When one's large-group identity is threatened, people will unconsciously and consciously search for chosen glories and chosen traumas and sometimes justify humiliating, killing and terrorizing the Other. At such times the interaction between the political leader and his or her followers becomes an important factor.

Twice in this book we have remarked upon Anwar el-Sadat's surprising and remarkable visit to Israel in 1977 and his speech at the Knesset. This is a very good example of how in history unexpected opportunities may arise to evolve peaceful interactions between opposing parties and tame or eliminate massive violence. Sadat's visit to Israel reminds us of Lord John Alderdice's key role in bringing peace to Northern Ireland. A psychiatrist who has also studied psychoanalysis, Lord Alderdice is a key member of the International Dialogue Initiative we described in the preface. He chose to get involved in politics and became a political leader in Northern Ireland. He writes: "During my time as a political leader in Northern Ireland I received hundreds of letters from people from different parts of the world who had the solution to the Northern Ireland problem. It was almost as though one day Garry Adams, Ian Paisley and the rest of us would read one of these proposals and suddenly realize that the author of the letter had a solution. Of course, this was never going to happen (Alderdice 2010, p. 19). Alderdice goes on to state, however, that in the context of a "talks process," a process of building relationships, even a rather poor suggestion can actually contribute to bringing peace. He describes how such a process started in Northern Ireland (Alderdice 2010). When Vamık Volkan and his interdisciplinary team from the University of Virginia's Center for the Study of Mind and Human Interaction brought together unofficial representatives of Americans and Soviets, Russians and Estonians, Croats and Serbians, Georgians and South Ossetians, and Turks and Greeks, they declined to offer solutions. Their aim was to start a series of unofficial dialogues and allow everyone to find, what they called, "entry points" for actual attempts for peaceful activities and agreements.

At the present time in many locations of the world people have realistic dangers and fears connected with international conflicts and terrorism, and these require realistic attempts for protections as well as for solutions. Realistic fears become complicated and more bothersome when they are contaminated with shared xenophobia, racism and fantasized dangers. We hope that this book is like a letter that was sent to Lord Alderdice with the idea that it contains sound ideas that can be drawn from if or when opposing parties sit around the same table. But, we also wrote this book for any reader concerned about increasing and spreading xenophobia.

Talking helps in understanding the surface motivations and sometimes the "psychic reality" of terrorists, but it is not advocating their horrific behavior. Scholars' understanding the "psychic reality" of terrorists is not enough. Whatever their ideology, deconstruction of terrorists' radicalized "bulges" is an aim toward a more peaceful world. Efforts, both violent and peaceful, for counterterrorism are also reviewed in this book. It is hoped that understanding the psychological and historical facts that are a part of human nature will be useful in dealing with the horrors that exist in our world now and especially with its increasing and spreading xenophobia. We will feel successful if this book helps the reader to separate real dangers from fantasized ones.

REFERENCES

Akhtar, S. 1999. *Immigration and Identity: Turmoil, Treatment, Transformation.* Northvale, NJ: Jason Aronson.

Akhtar, S. 2009. *Comprehensive Dictionary of Psychoanalysis.* London: Karnac.

Al-Adnani, A. B. 2014. *"This is the Promise of Allah."* Al-Hayat Media Center. https://ia902505.archive.org/28/items/poa_25984/EN.pdf

Allam, S. 2015. "Terrorists and their Quranic Delusions." *Washington Post,* April 10, p. A11.

Alderdice, J. 2010. Off the couch and round the conference table. In *Off the Couch: Contemporary Psychoanalytic Applications,* eds. A. Lemm and M. Patrick, pp. 15–32. London: Routledge.

Ali, T. 2001. "Former USA policies allowed the Taliban to thrive." *Turkish Daily News,* Sept. 25, p. 16.

Al-Qaeda Training Manual. 2000. [*Declaration of Jihad against the Country's Tyrants* (or: *Military Studies in the Jihad against the Tyrants*)]. English translation. Washington, D.C.: United States Department of Justice.

Anderson, B. 1991. *Imagined Communities: Reflections on the Origin and Spread of Nationalism,* revised edition. London: Granta.

Anderson, J. W. and J. A. Winer. 2003. Introduction. In *Psychoanalysis and History,* eds. J. A. Winer and J. W. Anderson, pp. 1–4. Hillsdale, NJ: The Analytic Press.

Anzieu, D. 1984. *The Group and the Unconscious.* London: Routledge & Kegan Paul.

Arlow. J. 1973. "Motivations for peace." In *Psychological Basis of War*. eds. H. Z. Winnik, R. Moses, and M. Ostow, pp. 193–204. Jerusalem: Jerusalem Academic Press.

ASDA'A. 7th Annual ASDA'A Burson-Marsteller Arab Youth Survey. 2015. Dubai.

Atkin, S. 1971. "Notes on motivations for war: Toward a psychoanalytic social psychology." *Psychoanalytic Quarterly*, 40:549.

Baader, A. 1972. Brief an die Deutsche Presse Agentur, 24:1. http:/socialhistory. portal.org/search/baader%20brief%20and%20der%%20deutsche

Balmer, R. 1989. *Mine Eyes Have Seen the Glory: A Journey into the Evangelical Subculture in America*. New York: Oxford University Press.

Barkey, K. 2011. "Secularism and its discontents: Politics and religion in the modern world." *Foreign Affairs*, 90:159–163.

Belasco, A. 2014. "The cost of Iraq, Afghanistan and other global war on terror operations since 9/11." *Congressional Research Service*, Dec 8.

Benmelech, E., E. F. Klor, and C. Berrebi. 2013. *Counter-Suicide-Terrorism: Evidence from House Demolitions*. Boston: Boston University Press.

Benotman, N. and C. Winter. 2015. *Islamic State – One Year On: Understanding and Countering the Caliphate's Brand*. London: Quilliam Foundation. 17 June.

Berman, E. 2009. *Radical, Religious, and Violent: The New Economics of Terrorism*. Cambridge, MA: MIT Press.

Bernard, W. W., P. Ottenberg, and F. Redl. 1973. "Dehumanization: A composite psychological defense in relation to modern war." In *Sanctions for Evil: Sources of Social Destructiveness*, eds. N. Sanford and C. Comstock, pp. 102–124. San Francisco: Josey-Bass.

Bloom, P. 2010. *How Pleasure Works: The New Science of Why We Like What We Like*. New York: W. W. Norton.

Bolitho, F. H., S. C. Carr, W. Chuawanlee, Y. Chaijukul, et al. 2003. "Poverty and economic crises." In *Poverty and Psychology: From Global Perspective to Local Practice*, eds. S. C. Carr and T. S. Sloan, pp. 205–225. New York: Kluwer Academic/Plenum Publishers.

Boot, M. 2013. "More small wars: Counterinsurgency is here to stay." *Foreign Affairs*, 93:5–14.

Boyer, L. B. 1986. "One man's need to have enemies: A psychoanalytic perspective." *Journal of Psychoanalytic Anthropology*, 9:101–120.

Brenner, I. 2014. *Dark Matters: Exploring the Realm of Psychic Devastation.* Oxford: Karnac.

Brenner, I. 2016. "The last witnesses: Learning about life and death from aging survivors." Paper presented at the European Society for Trauma and Dissociation (ESTD), Amsterdam, April 16.

Brown, J.A.C. 1963. *Techniques of Persuasion: From Propaganda to Brainwashing.* Middlesex, England: Penguin.

Buckman, J. 1977. "Brainwashing, LSD, and the CIA: Historical and ethical perceptions." *International Journal of Social Psychiatry*, 23:8–19.

Burleigh, M. 2009. *Blood & Rage: A Cultural History of Terrorism.* New York: Harper Collins.

Byman, D. 2011. *High Price: The Triumphs and Failures of Israeli Counterterrorism.* Oxford: Oxford University Press.

Cain, A. C. and R. C. Cain. 1964. "On replacing a child." *Journal of the American Academy of Child Psychiatry*, 3:443–456.

Caldicott, H. 1986. *Missile Envy: Arms Race and Nuclear War.* New York: Bantam Books.

Caschetta, A. J. 2015. "Does Islam have a role in suicide bombings?" *Middle East Quarterly*, 22:1–19.

Çevik, A. 2003. "Globalization and identity." In *Violence or Dialogue: Psychoanalytic Insights to Terror and Terrorism*, eds. S. Varvin and V. D. Volkan, pp. 91–98. London: International Psychoanalysis Library.

Chakotin, S. 1939. *The Rape of Masses: The Psychology from Propaganda to Brainwashing.* Middlesex, England: Penguin Books.

Chasseguet-Smirgel, J. 1984. *The Ego Ideal.* New York: W. W. Norton.

Cheour, M., O. Martynova, R. Näätänen, R. Erkkola, M. Sillanpää, P. Kero, A. Raz, M. L. Kaipio, J. Hiltunen, O. Aaltonen, J. Savela, and H. Hämäläinen. 2002. "Speech sounds learned by sleeping newborns." *Nature*, 415:599–600.

Crenshaw, M. 2011. *Explaining Terrorism: Causes, Processes and Consequences.* New York: Routledge.

Creutz, K., J. Saarinen, and M. Juntunen. 2015. Syrjintä, polarisaatio ja väkivaltainen radikalisoituminen. Syponur-väliraportti. *SSKH Notat – SSKH Reports and Discussions Papers.*

Davidson, W. D. and J. V. Montville. 1981–1982. "Foreign policy according to Freud." *Foreign Policy*, 45:145–157.

Dearden, L. 2016. "ISIS Yazidi sex slaves subjected to traumatic 'virginity tests' after escaping." *Independent*, January 30.

Delahunty, R. J. and J. Yoo. 2012. "From just war to false peace." *Chicago Journal of International Law* (Berkeley Law Scholarship Repository) 13:1–45.

Denton, D.A., M. J. McKinley, M. Farrell, and G. F. Egan. 2009. "The role of primordial emotions in the evolutionary origin of consciousness." *Consciousness and Cognition,* 18:500–514.

Dodd, V. 2015. Europol web unit to hunt extremists behind Isis social media propaganda. https://www.theguardian.com/world/2015/Jun/21/europol-internet-unit-track-down-extremists-isis-social-media-propaganda

Duke, L. 2006. Rev'd Up: Archbishop Desmond Tutu looks back, definitely not in anger," *Washington Post*, October 9. pp. C1, C8.

Dwork, D. 1991. *Children with a Star: Jewish Youth in Nazi Europe*. New Haven: Yale University Press.

Dyer, G. 2015. *Don't Panic: ISIS, Terror and Today's Middle East*. Toronto: Random House.

The Economist. 2015. *Islamic State. Spreading its Tentacles*. July 4, pp. 30–31.

Eikenberry, E., D. A. Weinberg, and J. Suzano. 2016. "The problem with Saudi Arabia's 'terrorist' re-education." *Foreign Policy*. February 16.

Elter, A. 2008. *Propaganda der Tat. Die RAF und die Medie*. Frankfurt: Suhrkamp.

Emde, R. 1991. "Positive emotions for psychoanalytic theory: Surprises from infancy research and new directions." *Journal of the American Psychoanalytic Association* (Supplement), 39:5-44.

Erikson, E. H. 1956. "The problem of ego identity." *Journal of the American Psychoanalytic Association*, 4:56–121.

Erikson, E. H. 1966. "Ontogeny of ritualization." In *Psychoanalysis: A General Psychology*, eds. R. M. Lowenstein, L. M. Newman, M. Schur, and A. J. Solnit, pp. 601–621. New York: International Universities Press.

Faimberg, H. 2005. *The Telescoping of Generations: Listening to the Narcissistic Links Between Generations*. London: Routledge.

Fonagy, P. 2001. *Attachment Theory and Psychoanalysis*. New York: Other Press.

Fornari, F. 1966. *The Psychoanalysis of War*. trans. A. Pfeifer. Bloomington: Indiana University Press, 1975.

Fowler, J. and S. Darren. 2008. "Biology, politics, and the emerging science of human nature." *Science,* 322:912–914.

Fox, J. A. and L. Levin. 2003. "Mass murder: An analysis of extreme violence." *Journal of Applied Psychoanalytic Studies,* 5:47–59.

Francis, D. 2004. *Rethinking War and Peace.* London: Pluto.

Freud, S. 1901. "The forgetting of names and sets of words." *Standard Edition,* 6:15–42. London: Hogarth Press.

Freud, S. 1915. "Thoughts for the times on war and death." *Standard Edition,* 14:273–301. London: Hogarth Press.

Freud, S. (1920). "Beyond the pleasure principle." *Standard Edition,* 18:7–64. London: Hogarth Press.

Freud, S. 1921. "Group psychology and the analysis of the ego." *Standard Edition* 18:67–143. London: Hogarth Press.

Freud, S. 1927. "The future of an illusion." *Standard Edition,* 21:5–56. London: Hogarth Press.

Freud, S. 1930. "Civilization and its discontents." *Standard Edition,* 21:59–145. London: Hogarth Press.

Freud, S. 1932. "Why war?" *Standard Edition,* 22:197–215. London: Hogarth Press.

Freud, S. 1939 (1940). "An outline of psycho-analysis." *Standard Edition* 23:211–253. London: Hogarth Press.

Fromm, G. 2011. *Lost in Transmission: Studies of Trauma Across Generations.* London: Karnac.

Gall, S. 2013. *War Against the Taliban: Why It All Went Wrong in Afghanistan.* London: Bloomsbury.

Glete J. 2002. *War and State in Early Modern Europe: Spain, the Dutch Republic and Sweden as Fiscal-Military States, 1500–1660.* London: Routledge.

Glover, E. 1933. *Sadism and Pacifism: Three Essays.* London: Allen & Unwin.

Glover, E. 1947. *War, Sadism, and Pacifism: Further Essays on Group Psychology and War.* London: Allen and Unwin.

Goodall, J. 2010. *Through a Window: My Thirty Years with the Chimpanzees of Gombe.* New York: Houghton Mifflin Harcourt.

Gregg, H. S. 2014. "Defining and distinguishing secular and religious terrorism." *Perspectives on Terrorism,* 8:36–51.

Greenacre, P. 1970. "The transitional object and the fetish: With special reference to the role of illusion." *International Journal of Psychoanalysis,* 51:447–456.

Grzyb, D.T., D. S. Fahmy, and D. Shaheen. 2015. *Daesh Information Campaign and its Influence. Executive Summary*. Riga: Stratcom.

Guevara, E. 1961 (2006). *La Guerra de Guerrillas* (Che Guevara, *Guerrilla Warfare*). Introduction by M. Becker. New York: Ocean Books.

Hafez, M. M. 2006. *Manufacturing Human Bombs: The Making of Palestinian Suicide Bombers*. Washington, D.C.: United States Institute of Peace.

Hammer, J. 2016. Is there a way to defeat Boko Haram? https://medium.com/@joshuahammer/is-there-a-way-to-defeat-boko-haram-2fa73a3b5b75#.nmvafc9mt

Harari, Y. N. 2014. *Sapiens: A Brief History of Humankind*. London: Vintage Books.

Hauser, M. 2009. "How nature defines what is right or wrong." Paper presented at University of Helsinki, Finland, September 2.

Hitler, A. 1925–1926. *Mein Kampf (My Struggle)*. Boston: Houghton Mifflin, 1962.

Hofer, M. 2014. "The emerging synthesis of development and evolution: A new biology for psychoanalysis." *Neuropsychoanalysis*, 16:3–22.

Hoffman, B. 2006. *Inside Terrorism*. New York: Columbia University Press.

Howell, W. N. 1997. "Islamic revivalism: A cult phenomenon?" *Mind and Human Interaction*, 5:97–103.

Iannaccone, L. R. 1998. "Introduction to the economics of religion." *Journal of Economic Literature*, 36:1465–1496.

İnalcık, H. 1987. *Fatih Devri Üzerinde Tetkikler ve Vesikalar (Documents and Investigations on the Era of the Conqueror)*. Ankara: Türk Tarih Kurumu.

Itzkowitz, N. 1972. *The Ottoman Empire and Islamic Tradition*. New York: Alfred A. Knopf.

Itzkowitz, N. 2000. The demonization of the other. (unpublished manuscript).

Jacinto, L. 2016a. "The rotten heart of Europe. The rampant dysfunction in Belgium puts us all in danger." *Foreign Policy*. March 23. http://foreignpolicy.com/2016/03/23/the-rotten-heart-of-europe-belgium-attacks-abdeslam-molenbeek/

Jacinto, L. 2016b. "Morocco's outlaw country is the heartland of global terrorism." *Foreign Policy*. April 7. http://foreignpolicy.com/2016/04/07/the-rif-connection-belgium-brussels-morocco-abdeslam

Jones, S. G. 2011. *Reintegrating Afghan Insurgents*. Santa Monica, CA: Rand Corporation.

Jones, S. G. and M. C. Libicki. 2008. *How Terrorist Groups End: Lessons for Countering al Qa'ida*. Santa Monica, CA: Rand Corporation.

Jost, J. T., H. H. Nam, D. M. Amodio, and J. J. Van Bavel. 2014. "Political neuroscience: The beginning of a beautiful friendship." *Advances in Political Psychology*, Supplement, 35:3–42.

Jowett, G. S. and V. O'Donnell. 1992. *Propaganda and Persuasion*. New York: Sage.

Kahn, C. 2008. *Undeterred, I Made It In America*. Bloomington, IN: AuthorHouse.

Kandel, E. R. 2006. *In Search of Memory: The Emergence of a New Science of Mind*. New York: W. W. Norton.

Kaplan, F. 2013. "The end of the age of Petraeus: The rise and fall of counterinsurgency." *Foreign Affairs*, 92:75–79.

Kaufman, N. H., I. Rizzini, K. Wilson, and M. Bush. 2002. "The Impact of global economic, political, and social transformation on the lives of children: A framework for analysis." In *Globalization and Children: Exploring Potentials for Enhancing Opportunities in the Lives of Children and Youth*, eds. N. H. Kaufman and I. Rizzini, pp. 3–18. New York: Kluwer Academic/Plenum Publishers.

Kayatekin, M. S. 2008. "Christian-Muslim relations: The axis of Balkans and the West." In *The Crescent and the Couch: Cross-Currents between Islam and Psychoanalysis*, ed. S. Akhtar, pp. 199–216. New York: Lanham, MD: Jason Aronson.

Kedourie, E. 1970. *The Chatham House Version and Other Middle Eastern Studies*. London: Weidenfeld & Nicholson.

Keegan. J. 1994. *A History of Warfare*. New York: Vintage Books.

Keeley, L. H. 1996. *War Before Civilization*. Oxford: Oxford University Press.

Kernberg, O. F. 1976. *Object Relations Theory and Clinical Psychoanalysis*. New York: Jason Aronson.

Kernberg, O. F. 1980. *Internal World and External Reality: Object Relations Theory Applied*. New York: Jason Aronson.

Kestenberg, J. S. 1982. "A psychological assessment based on analysis of a survivor's child." In *Generations of the Holocaust*, eds. M. S. Bergman and M. E. Jucovy, pp. 158–177. New York: Columbia University Press.

Kinnvall, C. 2004. "Globalization and religious nationalism: Self, identity, and the search for ontological security." *Political Psychology*, 25:741–767.

Kobrin, N. H. 2003. "Psychoanalytic notes on Osama bin Laden and his jihad against the Jews and the Crusaders." In *Psychoanalysis and History*, eds. J. A. Winer and J. W. Anderson, pp. 211–21. Hillsdale, NJ: The Analytic Press.

Kris, E. 1943. "Some problems of war propaganda: A note on propaganda new and old." *Psychoanalytic Quarterly*, 12:381–399.

Kris, E. 1944. *Radio Propaganda: Report on Home Broadcasts during the War*. New York: Oxford University Press.

Krueger, A. B. 2007. *What Makes a Terrorist: Economics and the Roots of Terrorism*. Princeton: Princeton University Press.

Landes, R. 2001. "Apocalyptic Islam and bin Laden." Paper presented at the Committee on International Relations, Group for the Advancement of Psychiatry (GAP). White Plains, NY. November 8–10.

Lappi, H., M. Valkonen-Korhonen, S. Georgiadis, M. P. Tarvainen, I. M. Tarkka, P. A. Karjalainen, and J. Lehtonen. 2007. "Effects of nutritive and non-nutritive sucking on infant heart rate variability during the first 6 months of life." *Infant Behavior Development*, 30:546–556.

Lasswell, H. D. 1938. Foreword. In *Allied Propaganda and the Collapse of the German Empire in 1918*, ed. G. G. Bruntz, pp. v-viii. Stanford: Stanford University Press.

LeBlanc, S. A. and K. E. Register. 2003. *Constant Battles: The Myth of the Peaceful, Noble Savage*. New York: St. Martin's Press.

Le Bon, G. 1895. *The Crowd: A Study of the Popular Mind*. London: T. F. Unwin, 1897.

Le Bon, G. 1910. *La Psychologie Politigue, et la Défense Sociale*. Paris: Flammarion.

Lebow, R. N. 2010. *Why Nations Fight: The Past and Future of War*. Cambridge: Cambridge University Press.

Lehtonen, J. 2003. "The dream between neuroscience and psychoanalysis: Has feeding an infant impact on brain function and the capacity to create dream images in infants?" *Psychoanalysis in Europe*, 57:175–182.

Lehtonen, J. 2016. "The matrix of mind: The networks of the brain, and the principle of transformation in art therapy for psychosis." In *Art Therapy for Psychosis*, ed. K. Killick. London: Routledge.

Lemma, A. and M. Patrick. 2010. *Off the Couch: Contemporary Psychoanalytic Applications.* New York: Routledge.

Lenin, V. I. 1906 (1965). "Guerilla warfare." In *Lenin Collected Works*, 11:213–223. Moscow: Progress Publishers.

Lewis, B. 1990. "The roots of Muslim rage." *The Atlantic Monthly*, September 20, pp. 47–60.

Lewis, J. 2005. *Language Wars: The Role of Media and Culture in Global Terror and Political Violence.* London: Pluto.

Lewis, J. 2015. *Culture, Media and Human Violence: From Savage Lovers to Violent Complexity.* London: Rowman and Littlefield.

Lifton, R. 1961. *Thought Reform and the Psychology of Totalism: A Study of Brainwashing in China.* New York: W. W. Norton.

Liu, J. H. and D. Mills. 2006. "Modern racism and neo-liberal globalization: The discourses of plausible deniability and their multiple functions." *Journal of Community and Applied Social Psychology*, 16:83–99.

Loewenberg, P. 1991. Uses of anxiety. *Partisan Review*, 3:514–525.

Lund, A. 2014. *Not our Kind of Caliph: Syrian Islamists and the Islamic State.* Washington, D.C.: Middle East Institute.

Lutz, J. A. and B. J. Lutz. 2008. *Global Terrorism.* New York: Routledge.

MacEoin, D. 1983. "The Shi'i establishment in modern Iran." In *Islam in the Modern World*, eds. D. MacEoin and A. Al-Shahi, pp. 88–108. New York: St. Martin Press.

Mahler, M. S. 1968. *On Human Symbiosis and the Vicissitudes of Individuation.* New York: International Universities Press.

Marighella, C. 1969. "Minimanual of the urban guerilla." https://www.marxists.org/archive/marighella-carlos/1969/06/minimanual-urban-guerrilla/

Mayer, J-F. 1998. "Apocalyptic millennialism in the West: The case of Solar Temple." Paper read at the University of Virginia, The Critical Incident Analysis Group (CIAG), Charlottesville, VA, November 13.

McCants, W. 2001. "Al Qaeda's challenge: The jihadists' war with Islamist democrats." *Foreign Affairs,* 90:20–32.

McCants, W. 2015. "Islamic scripture is not the problem." *Foreign Affairs*, 94:46–52.

McLuhan, M. 1962. *The Gutenberg Galaxy: The Making of Typographic Man.* Toronto: Toronto University Press.

Meinhof, U. 1971. *The urban guerilla concept.* www.germanguerilla.com/red-army-faction/documents/71_04.html

Meloy, J. R. and J. Yakeley. 2014. "The violent true believer as a "Lone Wolf": Psychoanalytic perspective on terrorism." *Behavioral Sciences and the Law.* Published online in Wiley Online Library.

Mitscherlich, A. 1971. "Psychoanalysis and the aggression of large groups." *International Journal of Psychoanalysis,* 52:161–169.

Mitscherlich, A. and M. Mitscherlich. 1975. *The Inability to Mourn: Principals of Collective Behavior.* Trans. B. R. Placzek. New York: Grove Press, 1967.

Money-Kyrle, R. E. 1941. "The psychology of propaganda." *British Journal of Medical Psychology,* 19:82–94.

Monti, A. 2015. *Punaiset prikaatit. Italian väkivallan vuodet 1970–1988.* Helsinki: Into Kustannus.

Montville, J. V. 1990. "The psychological roots of ethnic and sectarian terrorism." In *The Psychodynamics of International Relationships,* Vol. 1, eds. V. D. Volkan, D. A. Julius and J. V. Montville, pp. 163–180. Lexington, MA: Lexington Books.

Moore, J. 2016. "ISIS has destroyed the oldest monastery in Iraq." *Newsweek, January 20.* http://europe.newsweek.com/isis-destroys-oldest-christian-monastery-iraq-satellite-images-euroshow-417680?rm=eu

Morton, T. L. 2005. "Prejudice in an era of economic globalization and international interdependence." In *The Psychology of Prejudice and Discrimination: Disability, Religion, Physique, and Other Traits,* Vol. 4, ed. J. L. Chin, pp. 135–160. Westport, CT: Praeger.

Moses, R. 1981. "Dehumanization of the victim and the aggressor." Paper presented at the Meeting on the Middle East Conflict under the sponsorship of the American Psychiatric Association, Vevey, Switzerland. July 12–17.

Moses, R. and Y. Cohen. 1993. "An Israeli view." In *Persistent Shadows of the Holocaust: The Meaning to Those Not Directly Affected,* ed. R. Moses, pp. 119–153. Madison, CT: International Universities Press.

Moses-Hrushovski, R. 2000. *Grief and Grievance: The Assassination of Yitzhak Rabin.* London: Minerva Press.

Moyar, M. 2009. *Triumph Forsaken: The Vietnam War, 1954–1965.* Cambridge: Cambridge University Press.

Moyar, M. 2016. "The White House's seven deadly errors." Hoover Institution publication, Stanford University, February 12. <http://www.hoover.org/research/white-houses-seven-deadly-errors-0>

Muller-Paisner, V. 2005. *Broken Chain: Catholics Uncover the Holocaust's Hidden Legacy and Discover Their Jewish Roots*. Charlottesville, VA: Pitchstone.

Murphy, R. F. 1957. "Ingroup hostility and social cohesion." *American Anthropologist*, 59:1018–1035.

Neumann, P. R. 2009. *Old and New Terrorism: Late Modernity, Globalization and the Transformation of Political Violence*. Cambridge: Polity Press.

Neumann, P. R. 2015. *Victims, Perpetrators, Assets: The Narratives of Islamic State Defectors*. London: The International Centre for the Study of Radicalization and Political Violence, King's College.

Niederland, W. G. 1968. "Clinical observations on the 'survivor syndrome.'" *International Journal of Psychoanalysis*, 49:313–315.

Nussbaum, A. 1943. "Just war: A legal concept." *Michigan Law Review*, 42:453–479.

Ogunlesi, T. 2015. "Terror's nameless victims in Nigeria." *The New York Times*. Dec 2. http://www.nytimes/2015/12/03/opinion/terrors-nameless-victims-in-nigeria.html?_r=0

Olsson, P. A. 2005. *Malignant Pied Pipers of Our Time: A Psychological Study of Destructive Cult Leaders from Rev. Jim Jones to Osama bin Laden*. Frederick, MD: Publish America.

Olsson, P. A. 2014. *The Making of a Homegrown Terrorist: Brainwashing Rebels in Search of a Cause*. Santa Barbara, CA: Praeger.

Orbell, J. and T. Morikawa. 2011. "An evolutionary account of suicide attacks: The Kamikaze case." *Political Psychology*, 32:297–322.

Ornstein, A. and S. Goldman. 2004. *My Mother's Eyes: Holocaust Memories of a Young Girl*. Covington, KY: Clerisy Press.

Ornstein, P. and H. Epstein. 2015. *Looking Back: Memoirs of a Psychoanalyst*. Lexington, MA: Plunkett Lake.

Ortaylı, I. 2003. *Osmanlı Barışı (Ottoman Peace)*. Istanbul: Ufuk Kitapları.

Parens, H. 1979. *The Development of Aggression in Early Childhood*. New York: Jason Aronson.

Parens, H. 2004. *Renewal of Life: Healing from the Holocaust*. Rockville, MD: Schreiber Publishing.

Parens, H. 2011. *Handling Children's Aggression Constructively—Toward Taming Human Destructiveness*. Lanham, MD: Jason Aronson.

Parens, H. 2014. *War Is Not Inevitable: On the Psychology of War and Aggression*. New York: Lexington Books.

Perešin, A. 2015. "Fatal attraction: Western Muslimans and ISIS." *Perspectives on Terrorism*. 9:21–38.

Pinker, S. 2011. *The Better Angels of Our Nature: Why Violence Has Declined*. New York: Penguin Books.

Post, J. M. 2004. *Leaders and Their Followers in a Dangerous World: The Psychology of Political Behaviour*. New York: Cornell University Press.

Post, J. M. 2015. *Narcissism and Politics: Dreams of Glory*. Cambridge: Cambridge University Press.

Powell, J. 2014. *Talking to Terrorists: How to End Armed Conflicts*. London: Vintage.

Poznanski, E. O. 1972. "The 'replacement child': A saga of unresolved parental grief." *Behavioral Pediatrics*, 81:1190–1193.

Puckett, K. 2001. *The Lone Terrorist: The Search for Connection and its Relationship to Social Level Violence*. Washington, D.C.: Counterterrorism Division, FBI.

Purhonen, M., R. Kilpeläinen-Lees, M. Valkonen-Korhonen, J. Karhu, and J. Lehtonen. 2005. "Four-month-old infants process own mother's voice faster than unfamiliar voices-Electrical signs of sensitization in infant brain." *Cognitive Brain Research*, 3:627–33.

Rafiq, H. 2015. Foreword. In *Virtual 'Caliphate': Understanding Islamic State's Propaganda Strategy* by C. Winter, pp. 4–5. The London: Quilliam Foundation.

Rangell, L. 2003. Affects: In an individual and a nation. First Annual Volkan Lecture, November 15, University of Virginia, Charlottesville, VA.

Rashid, A. 2000. *Taliban: Islam, Oil and the New Great Game in Central Asia*. London: I. B. Tauris.

Ratliff, J. M. 2004. "The persistence of national differences in a globalizing world: The Japanese struggle for competitiveness in advanced information technologies." *Journal of Socio-Economics*, 33:71–88.

Reimann, V. 1976. *Goebbels: The Man Who Created Hitler*. Trans. S. Wendt. Garden City, NY: Doubleday.

Roberts, A. 2010. "Lives and statistics: Are 90% of war victims civilians?" *Survival*, 52:115–136.

Roy, O. 2010. *Holy Ignorance: When Religion and Culture Part Ways*. New York: Columbia University Press.

Salonen, S. 1989. "The restitution of primary identification in psychoanalysis." *Scandinavian Psychoanalytic Review*, 12:102–15.

Sandler, J. and A. Freud. 1983. "Discussions in the Hamstead Index of the ego and the mechanism of defense." *Journal of the American Psychoanalytic Association* (Supplement), 31:19–146.

Schützenberger, A. A. 1998. *The Ancestor Syndrome: Transgenerational Psychotherapy and the Hidden Links in the Family Tree*. New York: Routledge.

Shapiro, E. and W. Carr. 2006. "'Those people were some kind of solution': Can society in any sense be understood?" *Organizational & Social Dynamics*, 6:241–2.

Shengold, L. 1991. *Soul Murder: The Effects of Childhood Abuse and Deprivation*. New York: Ballantine Books.

Sivan, E. 1985. *Radical Islam: Medieval Theology and Modern Politics*. New Haven, CT: Yale University Press.

Smith, D. 2015. "Schoolgirls kidnapped by Boko Haram 'brainwashed for the group.'" *The Guardian* 29 June 2015. http://www.theguardiancom/world/2015/jun/29/schoolgirls-kidnapped-boko-haram-brainwashed-fight-group

Speckhard, A. and A. S. Yayla. 2015. "Eyewitness accounts from recent defectors from Islamic State: Why they joined, what they saw, why they quit." *Perspectives on Terrorism*. Vol 9, Issue 6:95–116.

Spitz, R. 1965. *The First Year of Life*. New York: International Universities Press.

Stein, H. F. 1990. "The international and group milieu of ethnicity: Identifying generic group dynamic issues." *Canadian Review of Studies in Nationalism*, 17:107–130.

Stern, D. N. 1985. *The Interpersonal World of the Infant: A View from Psychoanalysis and Developmental Psychology*. New York: Basic Books.

Suistola, J. and H. Tiilikainen. 2014. *Sodassa vieraalla maalla. Suomalaiset Turkin sodassa 1877 – 1878*. Jyväskylä: Atena.

Thomas, S. M. 2010. "A globalized God: Religion's growing influence in international politics." *Foreign Affairs*, 89.6:93–111.

Thomson, J. A. 2011. "Killer Apes on American Airlines, or: How Religion Was the Main Hijacker on September 11." In *Violence or Dialogue? Psychoanalytic Insights on Terror and Terrorism,* ed. S. Varvin and V. D. Volkan. London: International Psychoanalytical Association.

Thomson, J. A. (with C. Aukofer). 2011. *Why We Believe in God(s): A Concise Guide to the Science of Faith.* Charlottesville, VA: Pitchstone.

Thornton, R. 2009. *The 'Al Qaeda Training Manual': Teaching Terrorism.* Nottingham Teaching Resources. www.teachingterrorism.net/2009/07/11/the-%2%80&98al-qaeda-training-manual%E%80%99-not/

Tyson, P. and R. L. Tyson. 1990. *Psychoanalytic Theories of Development: An Integration.* New Haven, CT: Yale University Press.

UN Security Council. 2016. *Report of the Secretary-General on the threat posed by ISIL (Da'esh) to international peace and security and the range of United Nations efforts in support of Member States in countering threat.* Report S/2016/92. January 29.

Vander Valk, F. (ed.) 2012. *Essays on Neuroscience and Political Theory.* New York: Routledge.

Victoroff J., J. R. Adelman, and M. Matthews. 2012. "Psychological factors associated with support for suicide bombing in the Muslim diaspora." *Political Psychology,* 33:791–809.

Volkan, V. D. 1976. *Primitive Internalized Object Relations: A Clinical Study of Schizophrenic, Borderline and Narcissistic Patients.* New York: International Universities Press.

Volkan, V.D. 1979. *Cyprus—War and Adaptation: A Psychoanalytic History of Two Ethnic Groups in Conflict.* Charlottesville, VA: University Press of Virginia.

Volkan, V. D. 1981. *Linking Objects and Linking Phenomena: A Study of the Forms, Symptoms, Metapsychology and Therapy of Complicated Mourning.* New York: International Universities Press.

Volkan, V. D. 1988. *The Need to Have Enemies and Allies: From Clinical Practice to International Relationships.* Northvale, NJ: Jason Aronson.

Volkan, V. D. 1991. "On 'chosen trauma.'" *Mind and Human Interaction,* 3:13.

Volkan, V. D. 1997. *Bloodlines: From Ethnic Pride to Ethnic Terrorism.* New York: Farrar, Straus and Giroux.

Volkan, V. D. 2004. *Blind Trust: Large Groups and Their Leaders in Times of Crises and Terror.* Charlottesville, VA: Pitchstone.

Volkan, V. D. (2006). *Killing in the Name of Identity: A Study of Bloody Conflicts.* Charlottesville, VA: Pitchstone.

Volkan, V. D. 2007. "Societal well-being after experiencing trauma at the hand of *"Others":* The intertwining of political, economic and other visible factors with hidden psychological processes." In *Measuring and Foster in the Process of Societies: The Second OECD World Forum on Statistics, Knowledge and Policy.* Paris: OECD.

Volkan, V. D. 2009. "Some psychoanalytic views on leaders with narcissistic personality organization and their roles in large-group processes." In *Leadership in a Changing World: Dynamic Perspectives on Groups and Their Leaders,* eds. R. H. Klein, C. A. Rice and V. L. Schermer, pp. 67–89. New York: Lexington Press.

Volkan, V. D. 2013. *Enemies on the Couch: A Psychopolitical Journey Through War and Peace.* Durham, NC: Pitchstone.

Volkan, V. D. 2014a. *Animal Killer: Transmission of War Trauma from One Generation to the Next.* London: Karnac.

Volkan, V. D. 2014b. "Father quest and linking objects: A story of the American World War II Orphans Network (AWON) and Palestinian orphans." In *Healing in the Wake of Parental Loss: Clinical Applications and Therapeutic Strategies,* eds. P. Cohen, M. Sossin and R. Ruth. New York: Jason Aronson.

Volkan, V. D. 2014c. *Psychoanalysis, International Relations, and Diplomacy: A Sourcebook on Large-Group Psychology.* London: Karnac.

Volkan, V. D. 2015. *A Nazi Legacy: A Study of Depositing, Transgenerational Transmission, Dissociation and Remembering Through Action.* London: Karnac.

Volkan, V. D. 2017. *Immigrants and Refugees: Trauma, Perennial Mourning, and Border Psychology.* London: Karnac.

Volkan, V. D. and S. Akhtar (eds.) 1997. *The Seed of Madness: Constitution, Environment, and Fantasy in the Organization of the Psychotic Core.* New York: International Universities Press.

Volkan, V. D. and G. Ast (1997). *Siblings in the Unconscious and Psychopathology.* Madison, CT: International Universities Press.

Volkan, V. D., G. Ast and W. Greer (2002). *The Third Reich in the Unconscious: Transgenerational Transmissions and its Consequences.* New York: Brunner-Routledge.

Volkan, V. D. and J. C. Fowler. 2009. "Large-group narcissism and political leaders with narcissistic personality organization." *Psychiatric Annals,* 39:214–222.

Volkan, V. D. and S. Kayatekin. 2006. "Extreme religious fundamentalism and violence: Some psychoanalytic and psychopolitical thoughts." *Psyche & Geloof* 17:71–91.

Volkan, V. D. and E. Zintl. 1993. *Life After Loss: Lessons of Grief*. New York: Charles Scribner's Sons.

Waelder, R. 1930. "The principle of multiple function: Observations on over-determination." *Psychoanalytic Quarterly*, 5:45–62.

Weber, E. 1999. *Apocalypses: Prophecies, Cults, and Millennial Beliefs through the Ages*. Cambridge, MA: Harvard University Press.

Wessinger, C. 1999. *How the Millennium Comes Violently: From Jonestown to Heaven's Gate*. New York: Seven Bridges Press.

Wheeler, S. 2016. "Why has the world forgotten Islamic State's female sex slaves?" *Newsweek*, April 14. http://europe.newsweek.com/yezedes-islamic-state-christians-sex-slaves-human-rights-iraq-447842?rm=eu

Williams, S. E. 2015. "The bullied Finnish teenager who became an ISIS social media kingpin and then got out." *Newsweek*, May 5. http://europe.newsweek.com/bullied-finnish-teenager-who-became-isis-social-media-kingpin-and-then-got-out-328290

Winnicott, D. W. 1953. "Transitional objects and transitional phenomena: A study of the first not-me possession." *International Journal of Psychoanalysis*, 34: 89-97.

Winnicott, D. W. 1963. "Ego Distortion in Terms of True and False Self." In *The Maturational Processes and the Facilitating Environment* by D. W. Winnicott, pp. 140–152. London: Hogarth Press.

Wirth, H-J. 2009. *Narcissism and Power: Psychoanalysis of Mental Disorders in Politics*. Giessen, Germany: Psychosozial-Verlag.

Wood, G. 2015."What ISIS Really Wants." *The Atlantic*. March. http://www.theatlantic.com/magazine/archive/2015/03/what-isis-really-wants/384980/

Wrangham, R. (2009). *Catching Fire: How Cooking Made Us Human*. London: Profile Books.

INDEX

ABOUT THE AUTHORS

Jouni Suistola, PhD, studied history and social sciences at Oulu University. From 1968 to 1994 he taught at the Department of History, Oulu University, and between 1972 and 1994 he was the Director of the Open University Activities ("Summer University"). Between 1994 and 2013 he worked at Near East University, Nicosia, first as an Associate Professor and since 2001 as Professor of International Relations. From 1994 to 1998 he was the Chairman of the International Relations Department, from 1998 to 2008 the Dean of the Faculty of Economics and Administrative Sciences, and from 2001 to 2013 the Vice-President of Near East University. Dr. Suistola is the author of two books: *Kylmä sota paleltaa (The Cold War Makes You Feel Cold)* and *Kaleva. Sata vuotta kansan kaikuja (Kaleva. Hundred Years of the Echoes of the People)* and co-author of *Sodassa vieraalla maalla. Suomalaiset Turkin sodassa 1877–1878 (At War in a Foreign Land. Finns in the Turkish-Russian War of 1877–1878)* with Heikki Tiilikainen. He has also published forty-two scientific articles and hundreds of newspaper columns and articles. He has translated from English to Finnish four books on the history of warfare: David M. Glantz's *The Siege of Leningrad: 900 Days of Terror*; John Keegan's *A History of Warfare*; George H. Stein's *Waffen SS—Hitler's Elite Guard at War, 1939–1945*; and H.P. Willmott, Charles Messenger and Robin Cross' *World War II*.

Vamık D. Volkan, MD, DFLAPA, FACPsa, received his medical education at the School of Medicine, University of Ankara, Turkey. He is an Emeritus Professor of Psychiatry at the University of Virginia, Charlottesville and an Emeritus Training and Supervising Analyst at the Washington Psychoanalytic Institute, Washington, D.C. In 1987, Dr. Volkan established the Center for the Study of Mind and Human Interaction (CSMHI) at the School of Medicine, University of Virginia. CSMHI applied a growing theoretical and field-proven base of knowledge to issues such as ethnic tension, racism, large-group identity, terrorism, societal trauma, immigration, mourning, transgenerational transmissions, leader-follower relationships, and other aspects of national and international conflict. A year after his 2002 retirement Dr. Volkan became the Senior Erik Erikson Scholar at the Erikson Institute of the Austen Riggs Center, Stockbridge, Massachusetts and he has spent three to six months there each year for ten years.

In 2006, he was Fulbright/Sigmund Freud-Privatstiftung Visiting Scholar of Psychoanalysis in Vienna, Austria. Dr. Volkan holds Honorary Doctorate degrees from Kuopio University (now called the University of Eastern Finland), Finland; from Ankara University, Turkey; and the Eastern European Psychoanalytic Institute, Russia. He was a former President of the Turkish-American Neuropsychiatric Society, the International Society of Political Psychology, the Virginia Psychoanalytic Society, and the American College of Psychoanalysts. Among many awards he received are Nevitt Sanford Award, Elise M. Hayman Award, L. Bryce Boyer Award, Margaret Mahler Literature Prize, Hans H. Strupp Award, the American College of Psychoanalysts' Distinguished Officer Award for 2014, and Mary S. Sigourney Award for 2015. He also received the Sigmund Freud Award given by the city of Vienna, Austria, in collaboration with the World Council of Psychotherapy. He also was honored on several occasions by being nominated for the Nobel Peace Prize with letters of support from 27 countries. Dr. Volkan is the author, coauthor, editor, or coeditor of over fifty psychoanalytic and psychopolitical books including, *Enemies on the Couch: A Psychopolitical Journey Through War and Peace*. Currently Dr. Volkan is the President Emeritus of the International Dialogue Initiative (IDI), which he established in 2007. He continues to lecture nationally and internationally.